# Gideon: An Intimate Portrait

by
Audrey J. Williamson

Beacon Hill Press of Kansas City
Kansas City, Missouri

# Acknowledgment

Grateful acknowledgment is made to those who read the manuscript before its final form and who offered constructive suggestions for its improvement. These persons were Franklin Cook and Neil Wiseman, Joseph Williamson, Maylou Cook, and John and Chris Williamson.

Jacque Cork deciphered from my longhand and typed the first draft of the manuscript and Bonnie Wiseman did the final typing. To all of these persons I confess a debt of gratitude.

# Contents

## *Foreword*

This is the life story of Gideon Brooks Williamson, written by his wife, Audrey J. Williamson. It is not a biography in the usual sense of the word. It is rather a testament of devotion.

Gideon Williamson's parents chose his given name directly from the Bible. He was named for Gideon, the judge, whose story is related in Judges 6—8. Neither that story nor this is the recounting of a life entirely free from errors in judgment. But both depict a man of courage obedient to the divine voice.

So, it seemed appropriate to title this story simply *Gideon*. Phrases from the scriptural account of Gideon's life apply to that of his namesake.

Some illustrative passages follow:

*The angel of the Lord . . . said unto [Gideon], The Lord is with thee, thou mighty man of valour* (Judg. 6:12).

*The Lord . . . said, Go in this thy might . . . Surely I will be with thee* (Judg. 6:14, 16).

*The Spirit of God clothed Gideon* (Judg. 6:34, Hebrew).

*[In the battle the soldiers] cried, The sword of the Lord, and of Gideon* (Judg. 7:20).

# Introduction

Some years ago, I told Gideon I would like to write his memoirs. I thought I could make them something other than a saccharine eulogy of a beloved husband. I hoped they might have interest for people whether or not they had known him personally. I envisioned that they might have some value as written from his perspective as a participant in the making of the history of the Church of the Nazarene for 60 years.

Gideon poked a little fun at the idea at first, referring to it as his "Memoirs (pronounced mee-mors) and Remains." But in time his interest perked up and he suggested that I get at it. He even rejected the thought that I would have it published posthumously; he said he wanted to know how people would react to the reading of it. Perhaps he secretly chuckled over some possibly raised eyebrows. And on the last long drive we took in the summer of 1979, he did consent to let me carry along a tape recorder and especially while he was driving (he was usually asleep while I was at the wheel), we engaged in conversation and he recorded much of the material set forth in this volume. Some of the narration will appear in the first person as he related it. In some chapters, I have employed dialogue as we conversed together, and in some I have chosen to be the narrator.

In the fall of 1979 began his long and debilitating illness. I prayed earnestly and exercised all the faith I could muster that he might be miraculously healed. It was not to be. He would say to me sometimes, "Are you still going to write my life story?" And I always assured him that I was. But hands and heart were too full to begin the undertaking until he had gone Home on

December 30, 1981. Then, I felt too bruised to start. I shared my dilemma with my friend Louise Chapman. In her forthright manner she gave me the push I needed. "Do it," she said, "do it! And do it while your grief is fresh."

So here it is! I write out of my own inner urge to do so. And I write because I feel I have a promise to keep.

**GIDEON:** The Man
His Roots

# THE MAN

Gideon Williamson stood six feet tall. His body was well proportioned, his posture erect, and his carriage forceful. He moved with purpose and grace. His most striking facial characteristics were his blond hair and his blue eyes with their direct, sometimes penetrating gaze. There was a presence about him of which he seemed totally unaware. When he entered a room, he seemed to fill it, be it a hotel dining room, a men's clothing store, a camp meeting platform, a sanctuary, or a college chapel.

His voice was clear, well modulated, and resonant. It had a remarkable carrying quality. Listeners who suffered from auditory impairment often told him after listening to him preach that they had heard every word.

Bud Lunn, manager of the Nazarene Publishing House and his longtime friend, expressed these qualities well in a letter dated March 11, 1971, after Gideon had returned from preaching his father's funeral message. He said:

> My ol' General was in prime form, erect in his carriage, strong of voice, clear in thinking, and most of all, with that nebulous quality, "command presence," as we used to say in the army that a leader either had or he did not. Your message was superb and deeply appreciated by the family and friends.

Gideon's reactions in a given situation were immediate and, especially in his younger days, often explosive. No one ever accused him of riding the fence. But when he was wrong or had overreacted, he was quick to back up. He often said his reverse gears were in good working order because he had had to use them so often. This made it easy for him to forgive and to dismiss an unpleasant circumstance. Just two days before he died, his poor feet were so cold. I attempted to warm them with a heating pad and extra pillows. Somehow, my arrangement cut off the circulation and when I discovered it, his feet were blue. I was filled with remorse, immediately remedied the situation, then burst into tears. Out of sheer regret and frustration I cried, "Oh, I'm so sorry." Seeing my grief, he exclaimed with a measure of his old punch, "Don't be *funny!*" His rebuke was so characteristic, I was even glad afterward that it had happened. It was so like him.

He lived a disciplined life in every area. He exercised self-control in his eating habits. He required regularity of himself in taking rest and sleep. He was meticulous in keeping up his correspondence. When he had a task to do, he got at it. There was a memo on his chifforobe nearly every day he was at home. It might read something like this:

> Mow the lawn
> Get hair cut
> Make hospital call
> Write S. Y.
> Committee meeting at 3 p.m.
> File fingernails

And at the end of the day, the list would be checked and he would congratulate himself that he was up to date.

He authored several books, among them *Labor of Love, or Evangelism in the Local Church* and *Overseers of the Flock,* a heart-to-heart presentation on the pastoral office. Both enjoyed long and wide distribution. He also, at the request of the family, wrote *Roy T. Williams, Servant of God,* a biography.

Later he produced *Preaching Scriptural Holiness* and *Sermons for Holiness Evangelism,* and more recently *Models for Modern Ministers* and *Holiness for Every Day,* a day-by-day devotional book.

When the urge to write came upon him, he was tireless. He

had never learned to use a typewriter, but with a pad of legal paper and a pen, he poured it all out in longhand, often using his lap for a desk. Before he began to write, he had so thoroughly prepared and organized his material in his mind that it required only minor editing for publication. The compulsion to put *Holiness for Every Day* in final form was strong upon him. He gave himself unreservedly to the task until it was completed.

He prepared his sermons in the same thorough, painstaking way, writing them out in longhand, then striking off an outline which he committed to memory. It was his custom to preach from the pulpit without any manuscript except his Bible. The references he made to the Word of God had been committed to memory. Missionary Paul Hetrick told me once that in a single sermon of Gideon's he counted 72 Scripture quotations.

One day during his final illness, I thought of the files he had brought from Colorado Springs when we moved to Arizona. I asked him if we should not go over them while he was still able. His reply was, "Everything is in order."

He was a very private person and I took his word for it. But after he was gone, I opened the files. There were his sermons in longhand, alphabetized according to title. All in order!

He was disciplined in his devotional life. He gave himself daily to prayer and to the study and memorization of God's Word. He did this in private, but never did we neglect our family devotions. Even after the children were grown and gone, we observed this beautiful exercise morning and evening. I would not part with those memories.

He was an ardent believer in disciplined physical exercise. And though he never was a pro or anywhere near that, he played golf consistently for nearly 50 years. I have heard him say facetiously that his call to play golf was nearly as clear as his call to preach. It was in the early years in Cleveland when the pressures were crushing. He was experiencing great discomfort with nervous indigestion. I tried to help him with a careful diet, but he was getting little relief. One day while out in the car making pastoral calls, he was in so much pain that he pulled to the side of the road and parked the car for a few moments' respite. He was alongside a golf course, and it seemed an inner voice said, "That would help you." He bought a set of clubs the next day.

L. Guy Nees told me that many years later, following G. B.'s first trip to Africa, he came home and made an impassioned report of this visit to the General Board. He became deeply moved as he spoke and so did his hearers as he recounted the events of his 11 weeks on that great and needy field. Finished, he took his seat and slumped in his chair, spent with emotion. Then looking across the room, he spotted L. Guy and, suddenly coming alive, he "whispered" so that he was audible to all in the room, "And I played 90 holes of golf!"

He was generous with God, with his family, and with his friends. He carried a deep burden for the hungry and the victims of disaster and responded to their needs. Material possessions were to be shared. He never showed any tendency to grasp and hold them for himself. If dining out, he was quick to reach for the bill even when he was not the host, though I sometimes noted this habit didn't usually result in too much of a fight.

He loved people and was unusual in remembering their names and their settings. I recall that during the General Assembly in Dallas, after he had been retired from the superintendency eight years, on the Sunday following the Communion service we were trying to make our way through the crowd. The family had a reservation to eat dinner together, but Gideon was stopped so often I wondered if we would make it. I dared to remind him that time was getting away. I shall not forget his reply. "You go ahead. These are my people, and if they want to shake my hand and bid me Godspeed, that's more important to me than my dinner." We took our time and he got both—the loving esteem of his fellow churchmen *and* his dinner.

He especially loved children and young people and remembered their names and their faces. When we were being entertained at a meal in a pastor's home, he often pulled dollar bills from his wallet to express appreciation for the children in the family, and he was not deterred even when five or six children showed up at the dinner table. He loved to recognize special events in a young person's life with a gift, often a Bible.

Two years elapsed between his visits to Africa. But when he arrived at Council Meeting on the second trip, the teenagers crowded around him and he amazed them by calling out their names and identifying them with their parents. They even felt so close to him that two young fellows surnamed Perkins and Schmelzenbach succeeded in getting into our cabin one night and putting a dead lizard in his bed. He didn't mind the lizard; he loved the boys all the more for their prank. Later on, he was proud of the way these two determined to invest their lives.

Mealtimes were important in our family, and we made a supreme effort to keep them so. There was always food for thought as well as food for the body, and often before we had left the table some member of the family had been excused to get the dictionary, the *World Book,* or the atlas to prove a point. There was never any gossip or tale bearing. In fact, Gideon spared me as well as the children from any report that would be damaging to the character of a fellow member of the Body of Christ. We were often the last to know of a failure or a disappointment.

He was absolutely devoted to his family. He suffered over the fact that his responsibilities to the church kept him from home so much of the time when the children were growing up. But he never complained. We took my father into our home where he became our responsibility for the last 14 years of his life. There was never a moment of resentment or self-pity on

Gideon's part, and Papa Johnston loved him as a son. Gideon was the one I wanted to preach his funeral sermon when he died at the ripe old age of nearly 103, and it was an eloquent tribute.

Gideon deeply loved his two sons and his daughter. Their names were engraved on his heart. And they honored him in return. Their expressed comments on the occasion of our 50th wedding anniversary speak for themselves.

Joe's word:

The lines have fallen unto all of us, and especially to me, in pleasant places. I know I have a goodly heritage. I know that heritage has shaped all that I am. I know that it is our shared faith which now affirms that nothing can separate us from the love of Christ, and that in all things we shall indeed be more than conquerors. This day is the culmination of your strength, your gracious lives, your love. Love never faileth. It shall endure.

Maylou's word:

Fifty years! Fifty golden years! From my perspective, most of your years have been gilt-edged. I realize it is not because things were always easy—but you turned all things for good. Thank you for that.

Thank you also for being such good examples, in living, in doing, in loving. A quote from Faith Baldwin characterizes the impact you have made on me and my family. "Remember the good things and forget the rest and always try to understand."

"The path of the just is as a shining light that shineth more and more unto the perfect day." You have made my pathway bright and glorious because His light has shined through you.

John's word:

To honor you properly is impossible. But I hope you know how I honor you in my heart. I pray that I may also honor you with my life. Your strength of personality, your love for each other, your devotion to your family, your loyalty to your friends, your generosity to extremes, your unwavering commitment to God's kingdom, your faith and the communication of that faith to others are sources of inspiration for me. An ideal example set before me.

Your children rise up and call you blessed,
With more love than I know how to express . . .

Gideon was very proud of his seven grandchildren, and was grateful that four of them were nearby as the end time came. The whole family, 10 of us, had Sunday dinner together every week at our house during the last months of his illness, and as long as he was able we wheeled him to the table to enjoy the fellowship. This in itself represented what he often referred to as "the miracle." In our last move to Mesa, Ariz., we were aware that we would be living near our younger son, John, and his family. But we were amazed when a few months later our daughter, Maylou, and her family were located a block from our home. Her husband, Franklin Cook, had been appointed executive administrator of the Arizona Laymen's Church Planting Organization. And the "miracle" was further enhanced by the arrival of their daughter, Jacque Cork, and her husband, Mark, who took a position in youth and music with a nearby Phoenix church. I treasure this spontaneous tribute from Jacque, Gideon's first granddaughter whom he adored. Her name for him always was Gigi (G. B.). This is dated January 20, 1982:

Ma: [my pet name]

Since Gigi's homegoing, many beautiful tributes have been written about this great man of God and church leader. These have been wonderful tributes, all of them describing his abilities of leadership and strong character, while emphasizing his many attributes as a father and family man.

Now I think it's time for my tribute. When I think of G. B. Williamson, I think not of a general superintendent or a great preacher. He was all of these things, yes, but to me he was much, much more. He was my Gigi and I was his "pet."

I remember as a child running and jumping into his lap after dinner, waiting for dessert. He would pour coffee on his ice cream and I would be fed by his strong, gentle hands. Then he would whisper in my ear that I was his pet and he would tell me he loved me and give me a big "pear kiss" (a juicy one).

I remember riding Scatman, sitting in front of Gigi begging him to have Scatman canter (I called it a gallop then). The first time I ever "rode alone," I think I was about four years old and I stood on a bench at the estate and Gigi helped me on the horse and led me around. He was so proud that I took an interest in horses and always told me that I was a born horsewoman!

As I grew older, my childish adoration grew into real love and real respect. I remember one time after you had visited Nashville, I was about 14 and going through a rebellious stage. That visit was hard on you both, my mother said later, and after you left I got a letter from him telling me to, in essence, straighten up. I did!

One memory that will never fade is the time when I asked him if he would approve of Mark and me getting married on June 6, 1980. He was pensive, a bit surprised, and a little apprehensive, but he agreed. I'm so glad, though, that he told you he knew it was right. The prayer he prayed at our wedding was one of the most eloquent prayers I have ever heard and more important, I know it came from his heart.

These are but a few of my most treasured memories of my Gigi. Many more come to mind as I write this, yet I feel these are the most precious. I would feel honored if you would treasure this letter as I have treasured yours and if you feel low, reread this "tribute" and remember the way he was as I remember him—healthy, vigorous, and full of life and love.

Infinite Love, Jacque.

Though we were separated by distance many of the years of our married life, Gideon and I individually determined to keep close. We knew that took purpose and determination. For many years, we wrote to one another every day and sent a special delivery for Sundays. In the later years, when air travel became more feasible, he was able to come home oftener and spend more time at home. Among his effects, I found a message I had written for our wedding anniversary in 1953. It expresses the way I felt about him then and to the end.

> To my Darling—who for twenty-two years has been both husband and lover; whose constant thought and anticipation of every desire has been my continued amazement; who has joyously provided for every physical need, been the solace of my mind, and my spiritual inspiration; whose love has surrounded me as a garment and of whom I know I am undeserving; for whom every service has been my delight, and every expression of love, though inadequate, spontaneous and deeply sincere; who has always held, under God, undisputed sway on the throne of my heart, and who today is the center of my life. Your Audrey.

The expressions of his outpoured love for me are too poignant and too extravagant for this story, but shall be treasured as long as life shall last. They comfort me now.

Gideon had some funny little ways that in the beginning could have been irritating, but which actually became for me points of endearment. His ability to fall asleep wherever he was and in whoever's presence he was, is a case in point. I had to overcome my embarrassment and did so thoroughly that I even became defensive of him. I learned it was a lifesaver for him. When Morpheus beckoned, he responded. Then again, sitting on the platform in a large auditorium, he would shade his eyes with his hand against the bright lights and attempt to locate me in the crowded audience. I at last stopped feeling self-conscious and felt proud instead. I would even stand and wave to make it easier for him.

He had his little economies. He saved paper napkins and used them for Kleenex. Maybe it was a red one from the

Ramada, or a brown one from the Holiday Inn, or a blue one from the Sheraton. He would stuff them all in his pockets, then pull them out for display whenever necessity demanded. You should have seen the collection I pulled out of his pockets when he stopped wearing his suits!

We always made a great deal of Christmas, and Gideon was at the center of the activities. First came the family ritual of buying the tree and setting it up, then buying the oranges and nuts (his special chore), carving the turkey, and opening the presents. But he had a little way with his gifts. He would unwrap them, lift the edge of the box cover, and peek in, then close the box and put it on his stack of gifts. We had to guess whether it was a book, a shirt, a tie, or cufflinks.

His gift for me was always last and best—and always a surprise—a beautiful robe, a set of matched luggage, a riding outfit, or a fur coat. And he was almost as pleased as I!

I remember when Maylou and Franklin set December 23 as their wedding day, Gideon was impossible! "How could they do this to me, the mother!" A wedding two days before Christmas! Finally Maylou, who was able to read her dad like a book, asked me privately if I thought it would make any difference if they agreed to stay nearby until after Christmas dinner. I told her I thought it would make all the difference in the world. So she approached her dad with the idea of the wedding ceremony on December 23, the family gift exchange on December 24, the family Christmas dinner on December 25, and then the honeymoon trip. She caught him in the bathroom shaving, his face luxuriant with lather. As she talked, two big tears coursed down through the foam. He gave his immediate consent.

Gideon was fundamentally a positive person. I have some lines cut from a letter he wrote me when we were passing through deep waters. They are pasted in my Bible. They say, "Keep your heart joyful and your faith firm. All is going to be right. I love you beyond words to tell it. Your devoted G. B."

He had deep and abiding convictions, but he was able to recognize another viewpoint and to accept the will of the majority even if it ran counter to his own ideas. Then he could release the matter.

He had almost supreme confidence in the power of biblical preaching. When his own children were growing up and he felt they needed rebuke or guidance, he would sometimes say to me privately, "I wish I could *preach* to them," and he meant from the pulpit. This gave him divine authority. The theme he loved best and proclaimed most effectively was the message of holiness. This to him covered every area of the gospel spectrum; repentance, restitution, forgiveness, cleansing, growth in grace, maturity, Christian ethics, stewardship, discipling, missions—it was all encompassed in a life of holiness. Bill Sullivan, our former pastor and presently director of the Division of Church Growth, movingly paid tribute to this emphasis in a message to me dated December 31, 1981. He wrote:

> There seems to be a silence in the whole world. That clear convincing voice is quiet. That biblical voice, that holiness voice is silent.
>
> Yet, I know it was not simply the voice, but the person. It was the largeness of soul, the tenderness of spirit, the depth of compassion, the fire of zeal that made his message so powerful and appealing.
>
> It is difficult to accept the fact that Dr. Williamson is gone. There was always such a presence about him.
>
> You will be in my thoughts and prayers—and in my heart, Mrs. Williamson.

Gideon was able to master his moods. I could tell the kind of day he anticipated by the songs he sang in the shower or while shaving. Sometimes it was:

"Dare to be a Daniel, dare to stand alone"

or

"Jesus, keep me near the Cross"

or

"Give me, Lord, the mind of Jesus,
Make me holy as He is"

or

"Lest I forget . . .
Lead me to Calvary"

or

"Jesus, I'll go through with Thee"

or

"Oh, then to the Rock let me fly,
To the Rock that is higher than I!"

or

"Yield not to temptation!"

He was tough and tender, and he seemed to know when to be either. If one of the children had an accident or made a mistake, he never berated them when they were low, no matter how firm and exacting he had been in laying down the rules previously. He said to me once, "If helping the underdog is a sin, then I have a lot of sins to atone for."

The following letter from Homer Smith, an ENC alumnus and longtime pastor, illustrates the point:

January 1, 1982<br>Sweet Valley, Pa.

Dear Mrs. G. B.:

Our Jean called last night to inform us that your Beloved and our Great Friend has departed this life. Though I know for him it is far better, I confess it took me several hours to emerge from a deep sorrow. In many ways, Dr. G. B. was like a father to many of us.

You have heard that we first met at my father's church; Grand Island, Neb.—when I was in the fifth grade. With Willard B. Davis as his special singer, G. B. gave us a spectacular meeting. It was his personal invitation which propelled me to the altar, as it was his interest which sought me out when he came to be ENC's president. At every

24

meeting—college or district assembly—even general assemblies—he always gave me personal notice.

Today I brought from my file a "collector's item." Dated May 30, 1981, and written in his own hand, I read again his warm response to my congratulations on your 50th wedding anniversary. As you know, my father succeeded Dr. G. B. as pastor in Farmington, Ia. You can imagine the contrast . . . from a young bachelor Demosthenes to my "brush arbor" type father with a quiver full of little Smiths. The letter praised the stature and work of my dad. Nor did it stop short of saying helpful and uplifting things about my good wife and me.

Last time I saw my dear Friend was at Brooktondale Camp. A serious dysphonia was threatening to force me from the pulpit.

I broached my problem shamefacedly. Though I had drawn his fire other times, this time his great spirit enveloped me in a warmth of encouragement and healing. "You will finish your course with joy," was his parting word, after giving all the time I wanted. Those words have stood by me. And I am experiencing joy.

Please be assured of our prayers.

Every day he examined himself to see that he was "in the faith." He never allowed anything to remain a barrier between himself and another or himself and his Lord. He sought to exercise a conscience void of offence toward God and toward men. He lived by the admonition, "As much as lieth in you, live peaceably with all men."

One day in the latter period of his final illness, he appeared to be very pensive. At last I asked him what he was thinking about. He weighed his words. After a moment, he replied, "I believe God approves of the way I have lived my life." Perhaps he was already hearing the Master's "Well done, good and faithful servant. Thou hast been faithful over a few things. I will make thee ruler over many things. Enter thou into the joy of thy Lord."

# HIS ROOTS

Out on the freeways that summer of 1979, with the tape recorder on the seat between us and with the trucks thundering past, I said:

Audrey: Tell me about your dad.

Gideon: My father was Samuel Anthony Williamson. He was born on the 6th day of December 1849. His father, Thomas Jefferson Williamson, was the son of Dr. Anthony Williamson of Raleigh, N.C., who was married to Elizabeth Lee, a cousin of General Robert E. Lee.

My father's mother was Mary Spencer of Hartford, Conn. Her mother's maiden name was Mills and I am reasonably certain that the Samuel Mills of the famous Haystack Prayer Meeting, which was the catalyst for the American Missionary undertaking, was included in her family connection. Her father offered $100 toward their education to any of his children who would memorize and be able to quote the words of the New Testament. Mary Spencer Williamson qualified.

Audrey: I remember your daddy so well. He was a stockily built man with a ruddy complexion and white hair and a beard. Didn't some little youngster ask him on the street one year at Christmastime if he were Santa Clause?

Gideon: Yes, and he had a tender heart along with his rugged convictions. He was probably the most unselfish person I ever knew.

Audrey: Unselfish without knowing he was unselfish.

Gideon: Unselfish without emphasizing it. If anyone had to stay home when a trip was to be made, he was the one. If there appeared to be any lack of plenty in the food on the table, he was always last to serve himself. He was a man of impeccable honesty. According to his own word, he would rather be cheated out of $5.00 himself than to cheat anyone else out of a nickel.

Audrey: There is a story about his staking out a claim in Kansas.

Gideon: Yes, the government was offering land to anyone who would pay $1.25 an acre and live on it the major part of a year. So before he was married, my father filed a claim for 160 acres near Johnson City, Kans. He stayed long enough to take title to his land, but got lonesome and went back to the family in Missouri. Later, he decided this Kansas land wasn't going to be very profitable, so he traded his 160 acres to somebody for a donkey, then found the donkey was sterile and sold him for $2.50.

Audrey: Well, he didn't really qualify as a big-time financier, did he? But he left you a rich legacy in values that are imperishable.

Gideon: Yes, and I owe him and my mother a lasting debt of gratitude. My mother was Annie Marion Ellis. She was born March 12, 1860. She was 10 years younger than my dad. Her people came from Virginia to Missouri. She was reared in the Methodist church. But in her younger years, she came in touch with an evangelist, John P. Brooks, who was a leader in the thought and theology of the Church of God Holiness. She was sanctified under his preaching and since the Methodist church in her area frowned upon those who bore testimony to that experience, she identified with the Church of God Holiness.

In the days of Isaiah Reed's effective evangelism in Iowa, two girls who had come under his influence, Eva Axford and Maggie Stambough, came down into Missouri

in evangelistic campaigns and in one of their meetings, my
father was converted and sanctified.

Audrey: So they were both in the experience before they met.

Gideon: Yes, and I suppose that is what attracted them to one
another. I can't tell you the exact circumstances of their
courtship. My mother was living in Wellsville, Mo., and my
father near West Hartford. I do know that my father proposed marriage when he was past 38 years of age. After
some hesitation, my mother accepted. They were married
at 6 a.m. in Wellsville and left for my father's farm home
in a horse-drawn buggy. On the way, my father asked the
favor of a kiss and their lips met for the first time.

Audrey: How like your father you were!

Gideon: Wow! Is that the way you remember it?

Audrey: Not exactly, but I liked your way better. Now tell me
more about your father's religious background.

Gideon: His father was a Baptist and his mother was a Congre-
gationalist. Following in the Baptist faith, my father was
baptized through a foot of ice in his youth. I don't know
why he couldn't wait till spring. He attended a Congregational school at Denmark, Ia., in his teen years. However,
since my mother was a member of the Church of God
Holiness, he affiliated with that group also and they re-
tained membership there until many years later when
they joined the Church of the Nazarene.

Audrey: So your home always had a strong religious atmosphere.

Gideon: Oh, yes. My memories are clear of family worship both
morning and evening in addition to grace at the table at
every meal. I can see my father yet reach up every morning to the clock shelf to take down his spectacles and the
Bible. Then he would read from it and we all knelt and he

prayed. I can see him, now, looking out the window while he prayed.

Audrey: What were you doing?

Gideon: Watching!

Audrey: You formed the habit of not closing your eyes while someone else was praying very early, didn't you? You *are* like your father in many ways.

Gideon: I hope so! But let's get on with the story.

In the evening time, my mother read and prayed. I recall that I preferred the morning worship when my father was the leader because he didn't pray nearly as long as my mother did.

Audrey: And tell me about the atmosphere of your home. Was there sweetness and helpfulness? Was there strong discipline?

Gideon: Oh, there was that! My father was probably a little more strict and would have laid it on the line more insistently than Mother. My mother was very tender—very much a mother, very deeply spiritual, and known as a person of earnest prayer.

Audrey: I've heard you tell of her putting a shawl over her head—

Gideon: Yes, she would throw an old brown shawl over her head or shoulders and go out through the orchard to a quiet place to pray. If the weather was inclement, she went to a room in the house and closed the door. We all knew she was not to be interrupted. In Minnesota in later years, she would sit on the woodpile at night with the same old shawl drawn about her and watch the northern lights play. It was an impressive sight. She was a great lover of nature, of trees and flowers. In her later years, I can recall her going out before breakfast to cut a single rose so it could be on the table when we came to the meal.

Audrey: Tell me about your family meals. What did you have to eat?

Gideon: Of course, living on a farm, we had produce—butter, eggs, milk, garden stuffs. We always kept a good garden and had fruit trees and did our own butchering to provide our meat. Food was always abundant. Sometimes it was very plain. My mother was a good cook. She made biscuits every day. At least once a week she baked light bread and sometimes a pan of rolls. But brown-backed biscuits were the staple supply of bread at our table.

Audrey: I can remember your teasing her later on about having nothing to eat but—

Gideon: Hog jowl, cabbage, and cornbread!

Audrey: And I used to hear her protest, "Why, Gideon, we had pie and cake." And you used to say, "Not very often."

Gideon: Probably oftener than my memory recalls.

Audrey: You haven't said anything about the children. Your oldest sister was Mary; next, your brother Crawford, eight years older than you, and D. I. Vanderpool's close friend; then came your sister Callie and finally Gideon Brooks. You were named for the old preacher, weren't you?

Gideon: Yes, and for the Gideon in the Bible. I have several namesakes who took the name Brooks. Precious few, if any, choose to name their offspring Gideon.

Audrey: I have always loved the name—Gideon, "mighty man of valor."

Gideon: When I was a kid, if people would ask me my name I would answer, "Williamson." Gideon seemed so strange compared to Jack and Bill and Steve.

Audrey: Your mother got you up before the public early, didn't she?

Gideon: Well, in a way. My brothers and sisters were attending

Crabapple Grove School where all the grades were taught. I was too young yet to go to school, but my mother taught me a poem, "The Mischief Man," and somebody got the idea of my going over to the school to recite it on some special program. That was my first platform appearance.

Audrey: I suppose the "Mischief Man" was the devil! Your battle against his influence and power began early. Then there was another story about your precocity as a speller.

Gideon: Well, I went in to New Florence one day with my father to trade. I was possibly four years old. I saw a black man there and I went home and told my mother I saw a man who winked at me. She asked me his name, and I told her I didn't remember how to pronounce it, but I could spell it. I said, "It's spelled F-e-r-r-y-r-y." The man's name was Perry.

Audrey: No wonder you have been a good speller all your life! Now, your family moved to Minnesota for a time, didn't they?

Gideon: Yes, the year I finished the academy (high school) at what was then Central Holiness University, University Park, Ia. My father, having had some financial reverses, expressed a desire to accept a generous man's offer to buy 80 acres of land in Itaska County, Minn. That was in the fall of 1916. I was 18 years old and he asked me to go with him and I agreed. We lived in a log house on the shores of a lake. It was called Shallow Pond. It was about a mile from end to end. One winter I worked on the opposite end of the lake and used to walk back and forth.

Audrey: On the ice?

Gideon: On the ice! It would be 30 inches thick. In the early part of the winter, when the lake was freezing deeper and deeper, the ice used to crack and you could hear the sound from one shore to the other. One spring we helped a neighbor put up ice for the summer. We sawed ice blocks 30 inches thick and pulled them out of the water and stored them away in sawdust for summer use.

Daddy and I were alone for the first winter. Those were long days. I did not get work until the spring of that year, then I began to work for neighbors and received some financial income—very modest, of course.

Audrey: What would you earn in a week or a month?

Gideon: Possibly $50.00 a month, if I were working on a monthly basis.

Audrey: Were you logging then?

Gideon: That was the principal occupation during the winter in that part of the world. I cut down trees, sawed them into logs and pulp wood during the three winters I spent there. Then I drove a team hauling the wood into Orth, Minn. Of course, the winters were very cold there.

Audrey: How cold would they get?

Gideon: Down around 50 degrees below zero. I can remember more than once of rising in the morning, feeding and harnessing my team, going back into the house to have breakfast before daylight, starting out as the streaks of dawn were beginning to show, and it was 35 degrees below zero.

Audrey: Would you have to walk?

Gideon: You could walk or freeze. The team would keep on the trail or road. It was well marked and grooved. I would walk behind them to keep my blood circulating.

Audrey: You've always loved horses, haven't you?

Gideon: Yes, they say an old preacher by the name of Andrews was staying at our house when I was less than two years old. He picked me up and put me on a horse and the story is that I cried when they took me off. The horse's name was Belle. She lived to be about 21 years old. She was always a favorite of mine.

Audrey: I am so glad we were able to keep horses during the years we lived in Colorado and that I overcame my fear of riding so we could enjoy them together. Those are some of the happiest memories of our retirement years, riding out at the ranch in the flower-filled meadows or climbing the ridges or sauntering down the pine-bordered trail we loved so much. I am grateful for Mister and dear little Princess. What good memories! But back to Minnesota.

Gideon: I was up there three years. One winter I recall I worked for a man whose place of operation was about five miles from home, and I stayed during the weekdays there in a bunkhouse and slept among the other fellows that were engaged in the logging business. Of course, I did not use the same kind of language nor have the habits they had, so they called me the preacher.

Audrey: Did you feel lonely and isolated?

Gideon: Somewhat, but it didn't depress me. I kept a positive attitude toward life. I am sure it developed in me something of ruggedness and independence of manner in life and action. While I was working for this man five miles away, I made it home where my father and mother were every weekend. I would work a full day on Saturday, and after supper I'd take my lantern and walk the five miles home. I'd stay until after supper on Sunday night and walk back through the dark woods. My lantern was my protection. There were some bears, some large timber wolves, and quite a few coyotes. I'd often hear them barking over yonder in the distance, but I knew they wouldn't come to me because I carried the lantern. I learned then that if you walk in the light, you have more light. I learned later that the Word of the Lord was the lamp to our feet and the light on the pathway.

Audrey: Would you say those years up there were sort of "Arabian Desert" preparation for you, similar to Paul's?

Gideon: Well, hardly that. But it was a time for my stabilization and maturing. You see, my religious life in the early years was especially nourished at home. My mother played a reed organ and we used to gather as a family around the organ and sing songs, the old ones. "Nearer, My God, to Thee" was my favorite. Regular church attendance did not begin until we moved to College Mound, Mo., about 1905. Here is where I was first enrolled in school at McGee Holiness College in the grade department. There was an annual camp meeting held in the chapel of the old college building, and in a children's meeting there in 1906 I went to the altar and was converted.

Audrey: You were how old?

Gideon: Probably about eight. It was a very real experience to me. I still date my conversion at that time. During my teen years, I had some struggles within myself and was rather frequently at the altar during those days of very intense evangelism. Those in charge could count on at least one seeker in every revival meeting. But in my last year of high school, I made up my mind that when I went to the altar this time, it would be the last I would ever go as a seeker. C. W. Ruth was the evangelist. I did go to the altar and I kept my vow. That was in 1916.

After we went to Minnesota, alone I made a covenant with the Lord that I would live for Him and serve Him all the days of my life. This covenant I have tried to keep. During those years when I was working in the woods, I would go around looking at my traps to see if I had a skunk or a muskrat, and I felt sometimes as though I were actually preaching. I had no acknowledged call to preach, but texts would come to my mind and I would think of myself as being a preacher.

After my mother came up to Minnesota to live, she and I carried on a Sunday School two or three miles from where we lived in the Spruce Grove schoolhouse. Later a Nazarene church was organized there.

I went back to Iowa in the fall of 1919 to enter college at University Park, Ia., later called John Fletcher College. It was there that I made my choice and identified with the Church of the Nazarene. My brother Crawford had recently become pastor of the nearby Oskaloosa, Ia., Nazarene church. He and D. I. Vanderpool were both charter members of that church when it was organized about 1914. I became janitor of the church as a means of financial support and received $25.00 a month for doing so. That was my first job in the Church of the Nazarene.

Audrey: Crawford was in my class as a junior in Central Holiness University. He was respected most highly.

Gideon: Yes, his tenure as pastor of the Oskaloosa church was brief. In January of 1920, after conducting a funeral and burial service, He became ill with the flu which was raging at the time. It went into pneumonia and he died on January 29, leaving his wife of two and one-half years, Esther, and an infant son. My father was alone in Minnesota; Mary and Callie and I were all sick in bed with the flu, and only my mother was able to attend the memorial service with Esther.

This tragic experience made a very great impression on me, and I felt a deepening compulsion to live according to the will of God. I possibly had some talent for singing, and I had hesitated between becoming a gospel singer and a preacher. The call to preach became more urgent. Rev. L. N. Fogg came to hold a meeting in the church, and one day while I was doing my janitorial work, sweeping down the stairs, I was seriously thinking and praying about my life's vocation and the matter of preaching seemed to be borne in upon me very strongly. I said to the Lord, "If You would like for me to preach, give Brother Fogg a message for the evening that would point in the direction of a life consecrated to the Christian ministry."

Audrey: You really put out a fleece, didn't you?

Gideon: Yes, and it was definitely wet that night in the service. I remember walking down to the front to shake hands with Brother Fogg and saying, "I think your message tonight was for me." From that night, I began to think in terms of the ministry as my life calling.

Audrey: When did you preach your first sermon?

Gideon: Do you remember we had what was called the "Fletcher Conference" at the college where students called to preach could exercise their wings? Earl Milburn was the bishop of the conference, as we called him, and after I had confided in him some of my impressions regarding my call, he asked me to preach in the conference. I did on May 20, 1920, for the first time. My text was 1 Pet. 2:4. I can quote it: "To whom coming, as unto a living stone, disallowed indeed of men, but chosen of God, and precious."

Audrey: Well, you started with a big text, didn't you? And you have been finding and preaching from them ever since.

Gideon: My sanctification as a second crisis experience came soon after my brother's death. I was in a preservice prayer meeting in the church in Oskaloosa. Only a few were present. The Spirit came in no demonstrative way, neither did I bear any public testimony to His coming, but there I told the Lord I would accept His will for me whatever it might be. That commitment has been maintained at the deepest level for these many years. There came to me there a sense of light and peace that have grown brighter and sweeter as the years have gone by.

Audrey: Well, it's been quite a journey from the log cabin (two
rooms and a path) on Peach Hill in southeast Missouri
where you were born, to the present. But you can certainly
sing,
"All the way my Saviour leads me."

**Gideon:**     The Minister
                Pastoral Years
                Farmington, Ia.
                Chicago Austin Boulevard
                Cleveland First

# THE MINISTER

I have often heard Gideon Williamson say there was no promotion in the Church of the Nazarene from the pastoral ministry. He believed in the office and place of the pastor. He believed the pastor was the key man in every situation.

He had a shepherd's heart. He loved ministering to his people, getting to know them, sharing their burdens, helping them solve their problems, seeking out the discouraged or the straying among them and hopefully bringing them back into the fold. He was busy at discipling, finding new people, interesting them in the church and bringing to them the claims of the gospel. He was ever striving to feed the flock, leading them to green pastures and beside the still waters.

He would have been happy and fulfilled to remain a pastor all of his life. In fact, even after he became a general superintendent, he seriously considered accepting a challenging pastorate. Only the inner compulsion that he was serving where God had appointed him caused him to decline the tempting offer.

No duty was more sacred or significant to G. B. Williamson in his role as a general superintendent than that of the ordination of candidates to the office of elder. He knew that the majority of them would be entering the pastoral ministry. He was unwilling for this feature of a district assembly to be hurried or to be scheduled for an unimportant place on the program. It was to him a solemn and momentous occasion. Certain texts were favorites, among them: "The elders which are among you I exhort, who am also an elder . . . Feed the flock of God . . . taking the oversight thereof . . . Neither as being lords over God's heritage, but being ensamples to the flock" (1 Pet. 5:1-3). Almost without exception at his ordination services he called for the singing of

> *A charge to keep, I have,*
> *A God to glorify,*
> *A never-dying soul to save,*
> *And fit it for the sky.*

He was justly proud of the near 1,000 men and women upon whose heads his hands had been laid in ordination in this and in foreign lands.

He rejoiced that his three sons were all ordained to the Christian ministry. He dedicated his book *Models for Modern Ministers* to them, though John was quick to point out the fact that he did not mean to imply that *they* were the models!

A moving scene is etched upon my memory. John was ordained in 1978 by General Superintendent V. H. Lewis at the Northwest Ohio District Assembly. Among the elders whose hands were laid upon his head were those of his father, his brother Joseph, and his brother-in-law Franklin. That filled Gideon's heart to the brim. But when Dr. Lewis offered the credential to him to present to his son, it was almost too much. Overcome with emotion, he thrust the sacred parchment into John's hands and turned away. It was a moment too deep for words. A lifetime dream had been realized.

# THE PASTORAL YEARS
## FARMINGTON, IA.

Gideon's first pastorate was at Farmington, Ia., a town of not over 1,200 people in the southeast corner of the state. It was the second Church of the Nazarene to be organized in Iowa by P. H. Agnew, who was then district superintendent of all the midwest section: Illinois, Iowa, Indiana, and Wisconsin. Craig Weathers was pastor of the Farmington church in 1921. He planned to terminate his ministry there and wanted Gideon to come and spend a weekend with him and on the Sunday morning asked him to preach. The invitation was accepted. The text was "Follow peace with all men, and holiness, without which no man shall see the Lord" (Heb. 12:14).

And it came to pass that the church did call Gideon to be its pastor. It had been organized 12 years earlier with 36 members. According to G. B.'s own evaluation, it had had a "spectacular growth." There were 22 members when he took over! Craig Weathers had been loved and appreciated and had done good work, but he was only a part-time minister, since he was attending college.

When Gideon became pastor, it was understood that he would enroll in the college at University Park and make the 90-mile train trip to Farmington on each Saturday, returning to school on Monday. The train trips each occupied the better part of a day. Gideon attempted to utilize the time in study. He was to be paid $10.00 a week, $3.50 of this going for train fare.

After he arrived, he was informed that they only wanted him to come alternate Sundays. He was unhappy about that because he was eager to get something done and offered to come every week if they would only pay his car fare on the alternate weekend. But they were of a conservative state of mind and did not want to do that. So he went only every other weekend that first year.

The following summer, he scheduled a revival meeting in August. But a short while before the set date, the evangelist became ill and was forced to cancel. Gideon announced this to the church and the most enthusiastic man in the crowd said, "Well, that makes it clear to me that we ought not to try to have a meeting in this town. We have tried again and again, and we have never had any satisfactory results."

Gideon's reply was, "Brother, if I have to pitch the tent and do the preaching, the singing, and the praying myself, we're going to have a revival meeting in this town."

There was no reply. But they did go ahead. They pitched the tent down in the heart of town where everybody could see it. Gideon did the preaching for the first half of the meeting, led the singing, and sang some specials—believe it or not! The district superintendent, who was H. L. Kinsey, came and preached for another week. There was no great turnout, but an impact was made.

After the first year, Gideon went down every weekend. He often preached to as few as 8 people on Sunday night and to probably 18 to 20 on Sunday morning. The youngest person, a man who was most consistent in attendance at the church, was 35 years old. He taught an old man's class in the Sunday School and one of the dear saints taught an old woman's class and that was the Sunday School. There was no youth organization.

At the end of the first year, after preaching alternate Sundays, the district superintendent asked Gideon if he would like to stay for another year. His honest answer was, "I don't know that I can, Brother Kinsey. I have already preached everything that I know to these people." The district superintendent said,

"Well, the vote may have something to do with your decision."
As G. B. recalled, it was unanimous. So he stayed on.

At the end of the second year, they had another tent meeting on the school ground. There were three other active churches in the town besides a small Mormon group. The Nazarenes had called an evangelist from the East to come and do the preaching. He was very rugged. According to Gideon, "he had a Luther-like jaw but not a Luther-like brain." He tore into the other churches and ripped them up the back til they were up in arms against him. But he got the attention of the people of the town and some rose up in defense of the Nazarene church. Gideon cringed at the attacks he made on the other churches and didn't agree with all the evangelist said, but he tried to hold steady.

After the evangelist was gone, the little ministerial association that had been formed, and of which G. B. had been made secretary, met together to discuss whether to allow him to retain a place of office. They said, "You think you are better than we are. We don't know if there is a basis for fellowship with you or not."

"Well, brethren," Gideon said, "I recognize that you are all my superiors in age and experience and understanding of the Christian ministry. Of course, I don't do some of the things you do. Now there's Brother ———, he plays cards with his people, and I wouldn't do that; and Brother ——— takes some of his people and goes to the movies, and that I wouldn't do; and there's Brother ———, he doubts the deity of Jesus." (About that time, their eyes were popping.) "I'm just a green country boy, you know."

Then the Congregational preacher, who was the liberal among them, spoke up. "Well," he said, "I don't think we should deprive Williamson of membership in our association. Let's overlook all this. He doesn't subscribe to all the evangelist had to say and that clears him of responsibility for that."

So they allowed him to stay in the Ministerial Association of the city of Farmington, and to continue to serve as secretary.

About this time, the beginning of his senior year in college, he began to preach anywhere he could get his foot in the door. Many years later, after he became a general superintendent, I heard him describe the itinerary he followed. It was at a leadership conference in the old Kansas City First Church at 41st and Harrison about 1947. Gideon was pleading for evangelism. He said, "Why, if I lost my elected office tomorrow and had no pastoral pulpit to occupy, I'd *make* a place to preach. I'd go down the river to Croten and across the river to Athens and up the river to Bonepart. I'd go over to Possom Hollow and Mount Sterling and Clay Center. I'd go east to Primrose and over to Sharon Center and on further north to Salem. I'd preach at Dry Ridge schoolhouse and at Enbury Chapel and at Warren Baptist Church. I'd never stop!"

Dr. J. B. Chapman was sitting on the platform, and as Gideon's message rose in intensity, Dr. Chapman's shoulders began to shake with dry sobs so characteristic of him when he was moved. Afterward, he saw me in the vestibule; he laid his hand on my shoulder and said, "Oh, daughter, God was on him tonight."

I said, "Dr. Chapman, that's what he did when he was in Farmington. He did just like he said. Those were real places."

And Dr. Chapman said, "I know it, daughter. He couldn't have made them up that fast."

And from practically every one of those places people began to come to Farmington to hear him. He preached weekends, and often three times on Sunday, and the fruit of those years has scattered out across the United States to bless many areas while the fire has continued to burn these more than 50 years at the home base in Farmington.

Gideon had missed the district assembly in 1922 because he was down in Missouri holding a revival meeting, and he said,

"It seems more important to try to get some people saved than to attend the assembly." (Did he ever have to eat those words when he began holding assemblies himself!) But Dr. Williams was chairman that year and spoke a word of reprimand for young fellows that missed assemblies. And the next year, 1923, he was in the assembly. They were using one of those revolving cameras to take a picture of the crowd. Gideon was on one end of the line, and when the camera had passed him he ducked behind the group and ran around and appeared at the other end. So his picture occurred twice in that photograph. I told him if he could have known how many times he would have his picture taken in his lifetime, he could have spared himself the energy. He was valiantly trying to make up for the year he missed, I guess.

He graduated from college in 1924 and that was the year the church began to grow. In fact, he pushed himself to the point that he developed the first serious problem of nervous indigestion which plagued him more or less all of his life.

The Farmington church was host to the district assembly in August of that summer. H. F. Reynolds was the presiding general superintendent. Gideon said later he had no more idea of his responsibility as the entertaining pastor than the man in the moon. But with the kindness of the district superintendent and the secretary and Dr. Reynolds, who was always the soul of generosity and courtesy and magnanimity, he made it through. The assembly took an offering on the last Sunday for a proposed church building in Farmington. It amounted to a few hundred dollars. Gideon had been pleading and begging for a new church, and this gave him a little leverage.

They had worshipped from the beginning in a little brick church owned by the Christian denomination. The year before they had tried to buy it and thought the deal was completed. But a protest arose and the area supervisor for the Christian church came and told the Nazarenes they were going to reopen there themselves. G. B. said, "Well now, brother, will you notify us of your intentions to do this and that you would like us to vacate the church by a certain time?" He said a little reluctantly that they would do so, and they did. The Nazarenes had paid $5.00 a month rent for years on end and they owned nothing, not even the little wicker collection baskets nor the pedal organ that almost exhausted the little lady who had to pump it. They had nothing but a few dog-eared *Best-of-All* hymnbooks.

But enthusiasm began to mount; the board bought a fine lot one block from the center of town for $700 and paid cash for it. Pledges began to be made. There were two for $350 each. The pastor at Ottumwa, Ia., E. F. MacClaren, drew the plans and served as chief carpenter during the fall and winter months. They poured the concrete and fixed the cement blocks in it to form the basement. Gideon declared it will be there when Gabriel blows his horn. There was a great deal of donated labor. Dear Aunt Mary VonSeggen, who with her husband had given Gideon a home during the days after he finished college, loaned the church $1,000 so they could pay all their bills. The total cost of the building was $6,000. The church was dedicated in April 1926, by Dr. John W. Goodwin, who later ordained Gideon in 1927 at the district assembly in Marshalltown, Ia. Rev. L. N. Fogg, who had become district superintendent in Iowa, was also present for the dedication.

The church had begun to grow in the summer of 1923. Gideon's salary had been raised to $15.00 per week and was brought up to $25.00 a week by the summer of 1927. The Sunday School had over 100 members. Church membership had risen from 22 to 95. The attendance at the Sunday evening services was the largest of any church in town. Gideon began to feel that this was the time for him to acquire advanced schooling, and he wrote to E. O. Chalfant, who was district superintendent in Illinois, asking him if there was an opening in the Chicago area so that he might continue preaching and take advanced studies.

Dr. Chalfant invited him to come to the Austin Boulevard Church in Chicago to preach, and G. B. went. His text was "That in all things he might have the preeminence" (Col. 1:18). C. H. Strong, his predecessor who had announced his intention to move, remarked after the message, "This is your man."

Dr. Chalfant, in his characteristically shocking way, announced Gideon's acceptance of the call which he had subsequently received by saying, "This is what we're looking for on the Chicago Central, preachers with a crack in their tails, a crack in their tails, a crack in their tails!"

And so the move was made.

The church building in Farmington has been in continuous use from the day of its dedication until now. It is plain but substantial and has the appearance of a church that will remain.

I have heard Gideon say that the six years he spent in Farmington were the foundation for his total ministry in the Church of the Nazarene. When the time came for him to leave, he went off alone into the timber surrounding Aunt Mary's and Uncle Fred's brick house on the hillside and there struggled with his emotions. Then came the release. He squared his shoulders and went manfully to his new assignment.

# CHICAGO AUSTIN BOULEVARD

The next four years for Gideon Williamson were perhaps more significant in determining the course of his life than any other period of time. He was 28 years of age when he left the sleepy little town of Farmington to go to the great city of Chicago. He had been able to walk to most of his pastoral assignments; now he must spend hours on elevated trains and streetcars and buses. He knew Farmington like the back of his hand; now he must acquaint himself with the layout of the vast and sprawling city of Chicago.

A large YMCA was located a block from his church. Since he was single, here he roomed and boarded for four years. It was a sharp contrast to the gentle home life he had enjoyed with Uncle Fred and Aunt Mary VonSeggen and with his own parents who had come to live in Farmington the year before.

He enrolled in the Northern Baptist and Presbyterian seminaries where he encountered strong and sometimes liberal thinkers. He was exposed to influences he had only read about before. He felt the pull of strong personalities and received offers of places of service. Let him tell you about it in his own words.

"When I went to the Austin church," Gideon related, "the previous pastor told me there were two problems that had not been solved. 'One,' he said, 'we do not have an effective, well-attended Sunday evening service; and two, we have never had anything like a real revival that brought in new people and saw conversions at our altars.' While he was pastor," Gideon continued, "I had remembered reading in the *Herald of Holiness* a report which followed the usual format of reports for special meetings of the day. The only discrepancy seemed to be in the numerical results of the meeting. The report stated, 'We had a great revival which ended in a blaze of glory. We had one seeker, counting him as he came.'

"After I arrived," Gideon continued, "there seemed to be a new interest and attendance began to grow, and for many Sundays the little church was filled. Church membership grew during the nearly four years I was pastor from about 90 to 150. We had good revivals. I held one or two myself. We also had Dr. R. T. Williams and Haldor and Bertha Lillenas for a meeting which was a blessing. Unfortunately, Chicago streets were covered with ice the whole time. People who came to church came almost at the risk of their lives!

"That church had a real burden and vision for missions. They were always overpaying their General Budget. They assumed all their responsibilities loyally and faithfully.

"Some of the finest people I have ever known were members. Among them was the Garvin Family. Old Mother Garvin was a saint, a woman of great power in prayer and of strong and steadfast faith. Her son, George, was treasurer of the church and continued in that office for over 50 years. There were also Brother and Sister O. D. Like. They took me into their home and treated me like a member of the family. I could almost depend on it that if no one else invited me to Sunday dinner, they would. There was also J. L. Bush, a quiet man but of powerful influence in the church. Clara Langhouser, a member of the church, in the last year or two that I was there accepted a position as calling minister. She went to many homes and was a powerful person in influence and in prayer. She continued in that relationship until I left in 1931. The Meisterlings also were strong people.

"Others who added strength came from Chicago Evangelistic Institute, among them Elsie Blatherwick and John Swearengen. I became very well acquainted with Dr. Iva Durham Vennard, the founder and president of CEI. At one time, she let me know that if I would consider it, she would like me to become vice-president of the Institute with the intention that she step aside and encourage the board to elect me president.

"During my pastorate at Austin, John Thomas, evangelist, came to Chicago and established the Northwest Tabernacle and carried on an effective evangelistic program. When he left, Dr. H. E. Jessup came to take his place. We established a warm friendship. He succeeded me as pastor of the Austin church for two years, then resigned to become a full-time teacher at the Chicago Evangelistic Institute.

"During these years, I had the opportunity to preach in a union Thanksgiving service in the Congregational church, which was only two blocks from our own. Of course, I was frightened at the thought, but I did my best to be ready for the occasion; and when I stood to preach, I became conscious of the fact that the Spirit of the Lord was there to help me. This experience brought me to the attention of different people in that church. I had friends, too, in the great First Methodist Church of Austin just one block from my Nazarene church. I spoke on various occasions there, especially at the young people's groups and at special celebrations. On one occasion, when the pastor was gone, the pulpit committee asked me to supply their pulpit, so I took my congregation over there and did preach on a Labor Day Sunday. Again the Lord gave me freedom. Some time after that, the chairman of the Pulpit Supply Committee and the most influential layman in the church came to me at a time when their pastor had resigned and had accepted a call elsewhere, and with great seriousness said to me, 'Years ago a young man came to pastor our church by the name of J. S. Ladd Thomas. We got back of him and stood by him and he had a great ministry which covered a period of 12 years. We are ready to do that for you if you will give us the opportunity.' I did ask him what in the world I would do with my Nazarene church. He said, 'Bring them with you.' I remember saying I could not do that because that would mean I would be a traitor to my own church. But it was all rather consternating to me.

"Voices! voices! and they continued to call. Other churches asked if I would be available. Dr. Joseph Owen, president of John Fletcher College, my alma mater, talked to me unofficially about the possibility of coming to serve with him as vice-president, with the idea that I should become his successor. Exposure to the various brands of liberal Christianity rife in Chicago never appealed to me, but there was a time when I felt that possibly the intense program of the Church of the Nazarene was a bit narrow. I saw some things in the church that did not measure up to my own ideals of devotion and depth in the ministry and in dedication.

"My inner conflict was compounded due to some things I felt indicated insincerity on the part of leadership in our church. Some of the dear brethren of whom I was critical were extremely patient with me. I am everlastingly in their debt. I remember one time W. G. Schurman, the much-loved pastor of Chicago First Church, called me up and said, 'I want to come over and have lunch with you.' We arranged a date at his convenience and after the meal he came to my room and talked with me. Among other things he said, 'I like you and I know you are sincere and you have talent to dedicate to God and the church. But I'm afraid of you.' W. G. Schurman was a very conservative thinker, and I guess he feared the young whippersnapper might fly the track. Nevertheless, his interest and prayers were a strong influence to hold me steady in these days of crisis.

"The same was true of Dr. E. O. Chalfant, who was my district superintendent during the years I was in Austin. He had his idiosyncracies and eccentricities, but he was a wise man and he knew some of my conflicts yet he never took me to task for any irregularities he saw me practice. He was patient beyond any expectation that I might have had. Had those men landed on me and been critical of my attitudes and spirit, the course of my ministry might have been changed. But they were long-suffering and understanding and loved me and prayed for me. This has made it easier for me to be patient with young men who were not altogether established and gave evidence of that. I think in the years of my leadership in the Church of the Nazarene that young men felt this in me. At least I hope they did.

"An instance of the confidence W. G. Schurman placed in me is shown in the fact that in my first year as pastor of Austin, he asked me if I would help him do the preaching in a revival meeting. He had called the Vaughn quartet as singers and could not afford to pay them and an evangelist, too. He intended to do some of the preaching himself, but did not feel physically up to doing all of it. I agreed to go when he needed me.

"It was in one of those services when I had given an evangelistic message and a call to the altar that Paul Cunningham, Sr., who was far from God, was beautifully saved. He continued until his death to be a faithful layman in the church. This has been a bond of love between me and his family across the years, including especially Dr. Paul Cunningham, Jr.

"Among my warm personal friends during these years were two pastors, Lawrence Howe of Harvey, Ill., and Harry Morrow of Woodlawn Church, Chicago. He kept a personal interest in me and stayed close to me in a very helpful way.

"These years represented a time in my life when, as Dr. E. Stanley Jones put it, there was 'a traffic jam of wills.' But God knew my heart and recognized the fact that I wanted nothing but His will. After some months of struggle, I made up my mind that it was the Church of the Nazarene for me for life, and I made it known that I was going to put everything I had into the ministry of the church in Austin.

"Another problem confronted me. You must realize that during this time of struggle and uncertainty I was single. Audrey Johnston had not yet agreed to marry me. It was in 1913 when first we met. I was 14, she was 13. It was on the campgrounds of the Iowa Holiness Association at University Park, Ia. It was in a 'children's meeting' conducted by Miss Stella McNutt. (In those days, there were only children and grownups.) Miss McNutt had all the boys attending to preach a 'sermon' in the course of that 10-day camp meeting. I chose for my text, 'It is easier for a camel to go through the eye of a needle, than for a rich man to enter into the kingdom of God' (Matt. 19:24).

"The true and unromantic fact is that neither of us remembers the other. Comparing dates and times, we are convinced we were both there. Unquestionably we saw one another, I a lanky, tow-head in short britches, and she a shy girl with long braids. But we were neither one impressed by the other.

"We finished high school in the same year but in different places. In the fall, I went with my father to Minnesota. Audrey returned to University Park to enter college at Central Holiness University (later John Fletcher College). When I returned in 1919 to enter college, she was a senior. I asked her for the first date that fall. John Philip Sousa was bringing his band to the nearby town of Oskaloosa. She told me she planned to go with some girls. I quickly asked a good-looking blonde to go with me to the concert. And she accepted! But that was about as far as that went. I discovered early, however, the skill of using decoys.

"Following her graduation, Audrey remained at the college to teach in the speech department. I stayed out a year to work, but enrolled again as a sophomore in 1921 and finished college in 1924. This meant that I was a student in some of her classes and earned the right to refer to her as 'my old schoolteacher.'

"During these years, we dated occasionally, but we were

strictly 'just friends.' But the fall I went to Chicago to pastor, she
enrolled at Northwestern University in Evanston to work for
her master's degree. Since we had had a rather serious disagreement, I did not contact her for some months; but learning
through a mutual friend that she would welcome my attentions,
my hope and my courage both rose. Before summer we were
seeing one another regularly. She returned to University Park to
teach in the fall of 1928. We were corresponding every day. She
knew much of my inner struggles, and one day on a three by
five card she sent the following quote from Matthew Arnold:

> *Calm Soul of all things, make it mine*
> *To feel, amid the city's jar,*
> *That there abides a peace of thine,*
> *Man did not make, and cannot mar!*
> *The will to neither strive nor cry,*
> *The power to feel with others give!*
> *Calm, calm me more! Nor let me die*
> *Before I have begun to live.*

"These lines had a remarkable effect on me. I carried this
little card in my wallet for many years, and it is still to be found
among my effects.

"Our regard for one another deepened and I was ready to
make the commitment, but she hesitated. I knew for her it
meant changing denominations, for she was a Methodist, and it
meant giving up her career and adopting the life of the ministry,
so I tried to be patient. She was in Chicago in June of 1929
finishing up the work for her degree. She had been out to church
that Sunday, and we had spent the day together. She had gone
back to Evanston for the night, and before retiring I called her
up.

"In the course of the conversation, I told her I was like
Jacob. He served 14 years to secure Rachel for his bride. I told
her I had served 12. Then I added, but Jacob had a promise. And
then, unbelievably, she said, 'You do, too.'

"I said, 'Do you know what you are saying?' And she said, 'Yes, I do, and I mean it, finally.' I said, 'I'll be out tomorrow.' And I was.

"We both had school debts we wished to clear away, and she needed to fill the cedar chest I had given her with linens and towels and beautiful handworked pieces. But on June 6, 1931, on her parent's wedding day, when we stood and plighted our troth one to the other, it was for keeps. We both had reached a point of complete dedication, not only to one another, but to the full will of God as it should unfold for us. We plunged with heart, soul, mind, and strength into the new task before us— ministry to Cleveland First Church of the Nazarene."

# CLEVELAND FIRST

Several months before our marriage, the First Church of the Nazarene in Cleveland was left without pastoral leadership. It was Jarrette Aycock, evangelist, who suggested to Dr. C. Warren Jones, former pastor of Cleveland First and now district superintendent of the great Pittsburgh District, that Gideon be contacted. Dr. Jones got in touch with him and asked if he would be interested, and Gideon didn't turn him off. He soon invited him to come to Cleveland and speak in a Wednesday night prayer meeting. Gideon did so and preached that night on "God hath not called us unto uncleanness, but unto holiness. He therefore that despiseth, despiseth not man, but God, who hath also given unto us his holy Spirit" (1 Thess. 4:7-8).

The board nominated him then and the church called him to be their pastor. As happened in every move he ever made, he left the Austin church and the precious people there with deep emotion, but he felt clearly that he was answering God's call to Cleveland. We began our married life together in a new setting, which was good. The congregation looked me over with some scrutiny. One very strong lay woman who was a spiritual leader in the church told me afterward that when I went to the platform to be introduced that first Sunday wearing my going-away outfit as a bride, she said, under her breath, "My Lord and my God, what have we here?" But she added, the Holy Spirit immediately spoke to her consciousness, calling her by her full name, "——— ———, take your tongue off that woman! She's mine!"

And she was evermore my staunch friend. I have often wished in later emergencies that God had come to my rescue as effectively as He did that time. The people of the church did accept me and gave me a large place of service, especially among the children and teenagers, and among the middlers and aged as well. Some of the very happiest years of our lives were in those beginning years in Cleveland, and the friendships made solid at that time remain unto this day. When Gideon received me into the Church of the Nazarene, it was a moving experience for me. It was the climax of my total renunciation of the single life I had planned for myself. But G. B. got poetic and quoted Keats to say, "A mighty spirit moves within that narrow bosom," and the congregation snickered. It was disconcerting, but my lifetime commitment to be Gideon's teammate in the church of his choice was sealed.

The financial status of the church was very poor. A prominent member came to Gideon before he had accepted the call with a sheaf of papers letting him know that the mortgage on the church was $55,000 plus accumulated interest, with building operations notes still unpaid, and that there was a first and second mortgage on the parsonage as well. He made the picture as gloomy as he could. I guess he was doubtful that Gideon should accept the call, but it went through and he did accept.

The first task was to get the financial affairs of the church in order. He began to work at them as best he could, trying to keep all the creditors from losing patience with us. But Cleveland soon felt the full force of the great depression, and some of the most generous contributors to the church in other days were found to be on relief. The financial picture was grim. It was in the midst of this that the bank holiday was declared in 1933, after the election of Franklin D. Roosevelt as president. The bank that held our mortgage was never opened; they were paying their depositors 20¢ on the dollar.

Gideon conceived a plan for handling our debts to the defunct bank. I asked him many years later where he got the idea, and he said he didn't know unless it came to him from God.

The plan was that the bank would cancel all the accumulated interest the church owed on the first mortgage of $55,000 on the church, and that we would gather together by donation or by purchase passbooks of people that had deposits in the bank. We would then turn them in to the bank, thus hoping to take care of $35,000 of the debt with the accumulated value of the passbooks. This, if accomplished, would leave us owing $20,000 on the church.

When he first made the proposal to the bank directors, it was rejected. But a man in charge happened to be a man from Iowa, and he knew of Gideon's experience in Farmington. When G. B. told him of the plan and his rejection, he said, "Well, these (something like idiots) don't know a good proposition when they see it. Leave it to me." In a few weeks he informed the church that the proposition had been accepted. It had already been authorized by our board. We then went into the open market and bought passbooks at 15¢ on the dollar. These were from people who had already collected their 20 percent dividend from the bank. That meant they would be getting 35¢ on the dollar for their investment. We gathered enough to meet our proposition to turn over $35,000 to the bank in these passbooks. This was accepted as full payment. We then assumed the debt of $20,000 and began paying interest at 5 percent. This brought the debt to the place where it was manageable by the church. We cleared the debt on the parsonage, and the debt on the church was paid in full after our departure.

Not only were there financial problems to face, the morale in the church was low when Gideon became pastor. There were strong people of leadership quality and position among the membership who disagreed predictably among themselves. There had been some serious problems in the past that left prominent people under the shadow of improper conduct. But God began to work and help and new people began to attend the church and to seek the Lord. The Sunday School grew. The year we left, 1936, the average was 450. Church membership grew from 230 to 450. We had some fine meetings with such evangelists as Jarrette and Dell Aycock, R. T. Williams, and Paul Rees. Holiness conventions were an annual event with preachers such as T. M. Anderson and J. L. Brasher.

In the first district assembly in which he was present, 1932, Gideon was elected a delegate to the general assembly, which convened that summer in Wichita, Kans. The district NYPS convention elected him an alternate. Since all of the delegates to the general NYPS convention from the Pittsburgh District failed to show, Gideon was seated as an alternate. Dr. Reuben Gilmore was scheduled as a speaker on the afternoon of the second day of the convention. The preceding night, about 11 p.m., Dr. Aycock came to Gideon's room and informed him that Dr. Gilmore was not coming and asked if he would take his place the following afternoon.

The theme of the convention was personal evangelism. Gideon recalled a sermon he had preached recently on "I am debtor" (Rom. 1:15). He put together an outline and prepared his heart to preach. The Lord helped him. The next day he was elected general president of the Young People's Society.

I was not present. This was the first in a series of circumstances which prevented my being with Gideon at an important moment in his life, all of which transpired at general assemblies. In each case I was kept at home by one of the men in our family. This time I was awaiting the delivery of our first son, Joseph, who was born July 28, 1932. In every instance, I was spending much time on my knees in prayer, interceding for my husband, even though I did not know what was going on at the general assembly. Maybe God saw that my absence would thus prove more valuable to him than my presence. I have tried to believe that through the years.

Some prominent members of the Cleveland church were a bit resentful at the honor that had come to their pastor because they felt the new office would take him away from the church too much. He tried to avoid any crisis at that point. He did try to serve faithfully in both positions. This involved him in membership on the General Board for the first time. In 1936, he was reelected to serve four more years as general NYPS president. His message on that occasion was from Isaiah 12, "Cry out and shout, thou inhabitant of Zion: for great is the Holy One of Israel in the midst of thee" (v. 6).

His first foreign trip was made in 1939 when he and Dr. S. T. Ludwig went to Amsterdam, Holland, to the World Conference of Christian Youth, as official observers. Gideon's term of office as general NYPS president ended with the general convention of 1940 held in Oklahoma City.

Our Cleveland days were busy and happy. On August 9, 1935, we welcomed into our home and our hearts our second child, a daughter, Maylou. Joseph adored his baby sister and immediately became both protector and intercessor for her. Will Young, our Sunday School superintendent and faithful layman, walked through the parsonage one day on a carpentry job he was doing for us. It was feeding time and Maylou lay in the big chair fussing. Will stopped to comfort her, but she only cried the harder. Joe's sage comment, spoken so all could hear, was, "Never mind, little woman, he can't help it. It's the only face he's got." It didn't faze Brother Will. He and his parents, and in fact the entire Young family including Dr. Samuel, were our loyal and devoted friends and supporters from Cleveland days on. God bless the Youngs! I wouldn't have made it without Aunt Nancy's love and support.

Gideon's confidence in the power of preaching was demonstrated in Cleveland. More than any other factor, it accounted for the blending of spirits and the molding of personalities into a strong and unified body. He preached holiness and the power of the sanctified life. He preached a series on love; in fact, it so effectively worked in the life of one disgruntled member that he even said to me, "I'm getting sick and tired of this love business," before he finally accepted it as his way of life. Gideon preached a strong series on Old Testament characters. The spirit moved and there were seekers at the altars and the results were convincing.

Also, he lived close to his people. Calling in their homes was a regular part of his weekly schedule. I remember that very early in our days there, when he started out to spend an afternoon calling, the old schoolteacher in me spoke up and said, "Don't you think you should spend the time in your study?" His reply was, "When I mingle with my people first, then I know what to prepare to preach when I go to my study." He spoke to their needs because he was intimate with their problems—and I was convinced.

A final test came before our work in Cleveland was completed. The church, during the years of Gideon's pastorate, had no paid staff except the janitor, not even a secretary. Gideon wanted to bring in a man to care for the music at $25.00 a week. Some who had endorsed the volunteer leadership objected. The premature and unofficial announcement was made that the music man was coming. Unfortunately, the pastoral recall vote had been announced for the following Sunday, and the result was 27 negative votes for the pastor.

But even before he terminated his pastorate there, he had absorbed most of his opposition. Unexpected illness and accident in the homes of some of these people gave him opportunity to minister in special love and kindness to them. The healing came and as a result, the next pastor got a music director without any problem.

At the general assembly of 1936, the Board of Trustees of Eastern Nazarene College met and accepted the resignation of the then president, R. Wayne Gardner. They considered possibilities for the presidency and finally decided to offer it to Gideon. After some days of conference, discussion, soul searching, and prayer, he, with hesitation and reluctance, told the board he would accept the election and do his best.

This, of course, was the beginning of a new phase of ministry for him. The parting with the dear people of the Cleveland church was a wrench. But in August, the Grey Van was loaded and we were off on an adventure that was to occupy our lives for the next nine years.

O do not pray for easy lives. Pray to be stronger men! Do not pray for tasks equal to your powers. Pray for powers equal to your tasks. Then the doing of your work shall be no miracle; but *you* shall be a miracle. Every day you shall wonder at yourself, at the richness of life which has come to you by the grace of God (Phillips Brooks).

**Gideon:**     The Churchman
               College President, Eastern
               Nazarene College
               General Superintendent
               Foreign Visitation
               The Nazarene Bible College
               Story

# COLLEGE PRESIDENT
## EASTERN NAZARENE COLLEGE

Audrey: I have heard you refer to the nine years you spent at ENC as a "detour." I don't feel that way about it.

Gideon: Well, perhaps I don't either, now, looking at it in retrospect. The pastorate was always my first love and whenever I left it, it seemed to me then that I wasn't on the main road. But taking the presidency of Eastern Nazarene College was a compulsion with me. Humanly speaking, there was nothing to recommend my doing so. I was not in the dark when I accepted the election. I knew something of the problems, and in the final moment before I made known my decision to accept, I felt like I was standing on the brink of a pool of cold water, ready to take the plunge. I felt compelled to take that plunge. But I also had the conviction that God was able to help us solve the difficulties.

Audrey: Was the financial crisis the greatest one?

Gideon: Well, it certainly was the most imminent; the net worth of the college, that is, the difference between its debts and its assets, was $138,000. Total indebtedness was over $200,000, including principal and interest to the Granite Trust Company who held the first mortgage and on down to several current bills of less than $100 which had been standing for years. Included in this figure were annuities, life loans, and back salaries to faculty and administrators.

Audrey: What was enrollment in 1936, our first year there?

Gideon: It was down to less than 250 students, 222 I believe. We had been forced to adopt a stricter policy of admission as far as financial arrangements were concerned. Then, too, the country was still deep in the Depression.

Audrey: How did you begin?

Gideon: We had hoped with the money that came in at registration to start to satisfy some of our creditors. But before we could do so, the Ballard Oil Company, to whom we owed a sizeable amount for oil used in heating the previous year, put a lien against our bank account.

The Granite Trust, who held our big mortgage of well over $100,000, felt they had a prior claim because of delinquent interest, and they wiped out our bank account and applied it on back interest. Then they offered to loan us money on a note to replace the cash and help us operate.

Audrey: What did you do?

Gideon: I went to see the president of the bank, Mr. A. W. Martin, and he told me that to do so they would have to take a chattel mortgage on all our personal property. Every chair, table, desk, file, all laboratory and library equipment would be under chattel mortgage.

Audrey: Did the board agree to this?

Gideon: I called a meeting of the Finance Committee to consider this, and also to consider if it would be advisable to take friendly receivership. Our attorney, Mr. Arthur I. Burgess, a member of the Massachusetts legislature, had suggested the possibility and even offered to serve as the friendly receiver himself. But the committee voted unamimously not to follow this course but to try and work our way through. This, of course, was not easy.

Audrey: What next?

Gideon: The Board of Trustees had already voted to establish two bank accounts, one a special fund to be used for interest payments and capital indebtedness, and the other a current fund. There was no fixed educational budget from the districts allocated at this time. But such monies as came in from the churches on the zone were to be put in the special fund.

Audrey: You were walking a tightrope.

Gideon: By careful management, we were able to keep our grocery bills paid to date. We also paid off the Ballard Oil Company and gave something to our creditors on the basis of 30-day payments. If we did not live up to that, we were insolvent as far as credit was concerned.

Audrey: We must have talked about it at home, for do you remember my telling you that one night when Joe was saying his prayers, my mind wandered a bit with "Bless Mommie, bless Daddy, bless baby Sister, bless Grandpa ————," when all at once I realized he was pounding the floor with his little fist and saying, "O God, bless the special fund; O God, bless the current fund."

Gideon: Yes, I recall. He was about five years old. It was about the same time that he prayed for "Daddy as he presided over the Boston Multitudes." Well, we did watch carefully the possibility of an overdraft in both bank accounts. I remember the day I wanted to go see a creditor who lived down on the South Shore somewhere around Hingham. The school car was nearly out of gas, and I asked the bookkeeper how much cash was in the till. She looked and said, "One dollar." Well, I thought I would leave that for seed and went on.

I had done my errand and was headed back to the college when a sputter told me the tank was empty. I coasted down a convenient hill and up to the pump of a blue Sunoco station. I had one thin dime in my pocket. I squared my shoulders and said, "Ten cents worth of gas, please." Without a flicker, the attendant put in 10¢ worth and it got me home.

Audrey: That was when gas was a little cheaper than it is now. You probably got half a gallon.

Gideon: Well, they were great days. One good thing was that the government was helping students by paying them on a monthly basis for work they did on the campus. This gave us a little boost whenever the government checks arrived. It was understood that they would be applied to the students' accounts. Our credit rating improved, and by the end of the first year our creditors began to trust us. The bank holding the mortgage on the property and the chattel mortgage was also very friendly, and we tried hard to keep their confidence.

Audrey: What was your salary during these hard times?

Gideon: I believe the Board of Trustees voted to pay me $3,000 a year when I was elected, but if you will remember, I did not draw it. The faculty were so grossly underpaid and so far behind in salary payments that I wished to stand with them.

Audrey: Yes, and the faculty could all get milk and bread and canned corn and canned green beans and canned salmon from the kitchen pantry with our accumulated credit. I got to be an expert with salmon soufflés.

I remember our first Christmas. There was no money for gifts, but you went to the college bookstore and with your almost unlimited credit you got us each a present. You bought Joe the Ten Commandments on a plaque. You gave Maylou the little poem:

*Said the Robin to the Sparrow,*
*"I should really like to know*
*Why these anxious human beings*
*Rush about and worry so."*

*Said the Sparrow to the Robin,*
*"Friend, I think that it must be,*
*That they have no heavenly Father*
*Such as cares for you and me."*

And you got me a little plaque, "Jesus Never Fails." It has hung on our bedroom wall ever since. It is there now. I have read it a thousand times.

Gideon: Yes, He stood by us, didn't He?

Audrey: It was in that first year that God illumined the passage to me in Jer. 32:17, "Ah Lord God! behold, thou hast made the heaven and the earth by thy great power and stretched out arm, and there is nothing too hard for thee."

Gideon: Yes, from then on I had faith it could be done. [A cash report from Louise Dygoski, the bookkeeper, shows how bleak the picture was:

*Cash Report—May 6, 1937*

Current
| | | |
|---|---|---|
| Bank balance (May 5) | 21.13 | |
| Receipts | <u>13.00</u> | 34.13 |
| United Markets | | <u>47.76</u> |
| OVERDRAFT TODAY | | 13.63 |

Special
| | | |
|---|---|---|
| Bank overdraft (May 5) | 80.65 | |
| Deposit | <u>36.00</u> | |
| OVERDRAFT TODAY | | 44.65 |

Here's hoping that tomorrow's mail brings in enough to cover the deficit. This afternoon's mail brought in $5.00. I'm afraid that the city treasurer will demand some attention on Monday for we have received several notices saying that unless we paid our water bills by Monday, our service would be cut off. The bills for the three meters amount to about $190. L. D.]

Audrey: What about student morale?

Gideon: In the beginning it was very low. In fact, you remember I was away from the campus out on the zone that first fall when things got out of hand. The students had a protest meeting and destroyed some property. You let me know, and I came back to the college. In the next chapel service, I asked the faculty to absent themselves and told the student body: "If you don't expect to cooperate with the administration, you can go now and pack your trunks and go home. The administration will call the signals, or we'll turn the keys over to the Granite Trust Company and we'll all go home."

Audrey: Oh, boy! And Steve Bennett came down to the house that afternoon and told me about it. He said, "My first reaction was, who is he to talk to us like that? And then I said to myself, 'Well, he *is* the president.'"

Gideon: Yes, and Steve was loyal to me till the day he went to meet his Maker.

Audrey: Wasn't it in those days you organized the $10.00 Club?

Gideon: Yes, if a student was obstreperous, I fined him $10.00. Those very students became, in most cases, my most loyal friends. Several years later, when I was a general superintendent, I was under fire and was expected to receive a sizeable block of votes against me in the election. Prior to that, I was to speak on a given evening, and I received a note from "Mid" Wolf, Earl's wife, while I sat waiting on the platform. She wrote:

> Some of the old "Bender boys," the "Ten Dollar Club" and the "Fire escape artists" are in the balcony boosting and praying for you.

It warmed my heart and gave me courage. Mildred had been one of the fire escape artists in her student days.

Audrey: There were numbers in those years who went on to make us proud of them.

Gideon: Yes, Earl and Hazel Lee, Oscar and Marjorie Stockwell, John and Marguerite Nielson, Robert and Lois Nielson, Ken Persall, Wilson Lanpher and Gertrude, Doug Fisk and his wife, Rachel, and  Carl Crouthamel who made a brilliant record in the field of chemistry. Then in education there are Don Metz, Robert Sawyer, Bob Lawrence, Richard Howard, and many more.

Audrey: The faculty, too, was outstanding.

Gideon: They *were* outstanding. Dean Munro was a tower of strength. Knowing my own limitations in academic affairs, as soon as I arrived I had an official conference with the dean and told her that she would be responsible for the academic administration of the college. She accepted the responsibility graciously and proceeded to execute her assignment on sound principles. Ed Mann had a deep dedication to the work of the college. He assisted me as counselor and friend. In total, he gave 45 consecutive years to ENC from his days as freshman student to 22 years as college president. A record, I believe! Dr. James Houston Schrader, with a Ph.D. degree from Johns Hopkins University, came to be head of the Science Department at an amazingly modest salary. He filled an important place in the development of the college as member of the Scholarship Committee, in extending our publicity, improving our catalog, and in establishing and editing *The Christian Scholar,* the college paper.

    Dr. Stephen S. White was pastor and head of the Department of Religion in my beginning days. After four years, he left and Dr. Samuel Young, superintendent of the New England District, became pastor of the College Church and teacher of systematic theology. He followed me as president. He was loyal to the best interests of the college, financially, academically, and spiritually.

Audrey: Then there was Dr. Ralph Earle.

Gideon: He was head of the Department of Biblical Literature. When the seminary was established, he was chosen to serve on its faculty and has had a distinguished career.

Dr. Albert Harper was with us five years as head of the Department of Philosophy and Religion and went on to become editor-in-chief and executive secretary of the Department of Church Schools for the denomination, in which capacity he served with efficiency.

Other members of the faculty were loyal and capable and sacrificial to a superlative degree: Dr. Naylor, Prof. Alice Spangenberg, Mary Harris, Esther Williamson, among them.

Louise Dygoski was bookkeeper, and she was a life-saver. My knowledge of bookkeeping was extremely limited, but she knew what she was doing and was a devoted and hard worker. She probably experienced more than anyone else the trauma of those early days.

Audrey: You had strong support, too, from the Board of Trustees.

Gideon: Mr. Wesley Angel was very helpful. He was a wise counselor and very valuable in matters of building and finance. He was thoroughly loyal. The whole board was very understanding, patient, supportive, and sympathetic. Dr. C. Warren Jones was chairman for a year or more until he was elected to the office of secretary of the Department of Foreign Missions. He promoted the idea that the districts should support the college with regular financial payments. I want to pay tribute, too, to Evangelist Martha Curry. Her support was unofficial, but she carried the burden of ENC for many years and was wise in counsel and strong in encouragement.

Audrey: What do you consider the outstanding accomplishments of your nine years at ENC?

Gideon: We were able to pay all current and capital indebtedness, leaving as liabilities only a few small life loans and annuities. A mortgage-burning ceremony was held on the steps of the Administration Building on a chilly New England June day in 1944. Rev. John Nielson, then district superintendent of the New England District, had prepared a wooden bowl in which to burn the mortgage. It was signed by members of the board and is still in our possession. The choir sang "A Mighty Fortress Is Our God" under Mrs. Esther Williamson's direction. Dr. J. Glenn Gould gave the principal address. There were other speeches appropriate to the occasion, among them one by Mr. Delcivar King, chairman of the board of the Granite Trust Company. He was an interesting man of great understanding and especially skillful in matters of finance. He said, "I am glad! and I am sad! I am glad for the college that their financial affairs have greatly improved in recent years. And I am sad for the Granite Trust Company which will be losing interest on a loan that has been very satisfactory of late!"

[A letter from W. J. Martin, president of the Granite Trust Company, adds an official word of commendation:

March 14, 1946

TO WHOM IT MAY CONCERN:

Our relationship with the Eastern Nazarene College during the period the Reverend Gideon B. Williamson was its president and directing head was most satisfactory.

Consistent improvement was made in the college's finances as evidenced by the amortization of the mortgage held by us on the property, which mortgage was quite steadily reduced from an amount in excess of $100,000 in 1936 until paid off in 1944. Unsecured loans during these years, never excessive, were taken care of satisfactorily and such reports as came to us from time to time indicate that similar improvement was made in the discharging of local trade obligations. We believe this record bespeaks sound and progressive management.

75

The Reverend Williamson took over a most difficult situation but by his apparent ability to radiate enthusiasm and confidence was able to accomplish much.

In 1941 and 1942, after surveys made by the Department of Education, we believe the college was granted permission to confer the degree of Bachelor of Science, Bachelor of Theology, Bachelor of Arts and Theology, and was also invited to membership in the New England Association of Colleges and Secondary Schools.

In our opinion, this progress was made possible by the personality, efficiency, and sound administrative qualities of its president.

Very truly yours,
/s/ William J. Martin
William J. Martin, President]

Gideon: In the accreditation by the New England Association of Colleges and Secondary Schools and by the Association of American Colleges and Universities, Dean Munro and Dr. Schrader played an important part.

Audrey: It didn't happen all at once, did it?

Gideon: No, it was a long and painful process and meant raising additional funds to improve our library and science laboratories as well as strengthen our curriculum. We had Uncle Bud Robinson for a tour and he succeeded in raising more than the magnificent sum of $10,000, which was our aim. We kept working toward our goals.

We brought our appeals several times to the examining board and one year were very hopeful of a favorable response. It met with further postponement. During this time of stress, faculty and students kept very supportive and hopeful in attitude and finally the recognition we sought was gained.

Audrey: I think I remember most of all the improvement in morale.

Gideon: Yes, on the part of the students and faculty and in the decided change in attitude of district leaders and pastors across the zone.

Student enrollment from 1936-37 to 1944-45 practically doubled. And these were depression and war years. We sought to keep spiritual interests in their rightful place. Every class opened with prayer. Every day of the week except one there was a chapel service. There was an opening convention every year and a revival of a week's duration in each term. We sought earnestly to relate the college to the purpose of the Church of the Nazarene. Preacher training was important and had first place in our program and curriculum. We had such outstanding speakers for revivals as Jarrette and Dell Aycock, Dr. Hardy C. Powers, J. H. Parker, Martha Curry, A. B. Carey, Dr. J. Glenn Gould.

Audrey: I have been thinking while we were reviewing these ENC days of an incident that occurred on shipboard when you were taking a foreign trip alone as a general superintendent.

Your deck chair was adjacent to those of a group of five or six people traveling together. They had conversed with you some and had observed you. On the last day out, one of the group said, "Mr. Williamson, we have been guessing what your profession is and we haven't agreed on anything. One of us thinks you are in finance; maybe a banker; one of us says you are in public relations, you deal with people. Another one of us thinks you are in education, maybe a teacher, a speaker of some sort; and one of us says you must be in the diplomatic service. Mr. Williamson, what is your business?"

Gideon: I replied, "I am a preacher of the gospel!"

Audrey: Maybe if they could have known your record at ENC, they would have decided they were all right: financier,

public relations man, diplomat, speaker, but foremost and
always—a preacher of the gospel.
*Teach us, good Lord, to serve Thee as Thou deservest:*
*to give and not to count the cost;*
*to fight and not to heed the wounds;*
*to toil and not to seek for rest;*
*to labor and not ask for any reward,*
*save that of knowing that we do Thy will.*
*Amen*

—Ignatius Loyola

# GENERAL SUPERINTENDENT

It seems appropriate that Gideon tell you in his own words of the events that led up to his election as a general superintendent. The General Assembly of 1944 was the second time in his official career that the men of our family prevented me from being with my husband at a time when he needed me very much. I was in Wollaston awaiting the arrival of our son John who was born August 1. However, as before, I was much in prayer for him. This is the story as he recounts it:

"I went to the General Assembly in Minneapolis in 1944 at the end of eight years of service at ENC. I had been invited to give the keynote address on the first night of the NYPS convention. My theme was 'Jesus, the Light of the World.' My text was, 'As long as I am in the world, I am the light of the world. . . . he that followeth me shall not walk in darkness, but shall have the light of life' (John 9:5; 8:12). I prepared faithfully and the Lord helped me deliver the message with blessing. There was an enthusiastic response on the part of the congregation.

"The election of general superintendents was early on the docket of the General Assembly. Incumbents Williams, Chapman, and Miller were reelected. Dr. O. J. Nease was not reelected. He did retain a substantial block of votes and continued in the running for three ballots. After the third ballot was taken, the assembly was adjourned at 12 noon not to meet again until 7:00 that evening.

"When we reconvened and the board of tellers reported, Dr.

Nease had not gained enough votes for relection. He graciously withdrew saying, 'The church can get along without me, but I can't get along without the church.'

"On the first ballot, I had received 125 votes for general superintendent. On the fourth ballot, I had 198. After the withdrawal of Dr. Nease, his support turned to Dr. Hardy C. Powers and he was elected on the eighth ballot. I never questioned the providential ordering of the election of Dr. Powers. He served in a time of our church's history when his spirit and understanding of people on all levels of leadership were needed. He served with distinction for 24 years.

"The quadrennium that followed was momentous. In the first year, the seminary was established and Dr. Hugh C. Benner, pastor of Kansas City First Church, was elected president. Dr. Jarrette Aycock, who was superintendent of the Kansas City District, contacted me and asked me if I would consider the pastorate of First Church. After prayerful consideration, I allowed my name to be presented. I was nominated by the board and called by the church. I accepted with the thought that I would continue in pastoral ministry the rest of my life. We closed our years of service at ENC with the commencement season of 1945 and began immediately in the pastorate of Kansas City First Church. I was exceedingly happy there and was well received. It was the beginning year of the seminary and of the radio league, as it was then called.

"Another event of lasting importance was the initiation of the Spanish Department in 1946 under Dr. Honorato Reza. This resulted in the development of literature for international consumption that grew to be the largest production of holiness literature in non-English languages.

"These things brought to Kansas City some very able people, practically all of whom became members of First Church. During the year I received 158 members, some 40 by profession of faith and others by transfer. It was an exciting experience to preach to the seminary faculty and the students also, in considerable numbers, identified with First Church as members.

"In the fall of 1945, Dr. R. T. Williams, after finishing his assembly schedule, had a massive stroke in Columbus, Ga., and struggled to regain his health until March of 1946. On the 25th of that month, he was called to his eternal reward after having served the church as a general superintendent in its most critical period of progress. Dr. Chapman said at his funeral that he had for 30 years 'marched at the head of the Nazarene column.'

"On the death of Dr. Williams, at the request of the family I took charge of the funeral and brought the message. God especially helped me. The tributes paid Dr. Williams were eloquent. A bank of flowers eight feet wide reached across the front of the church at 41st and Harrison where the funeral was held.

"Before he left Kansas City, Dr. Chapman announced that following *Manual* procedure, an election would be held to fill the vacancy on the Board of General Superintendents caused by the death of Dr. Williams. Upon recommendation of the general superintendents, the district superintendents would cast a ballot by mail and continue to ballot until a general superintendent had been elected.

"On the first ballot, I had more than half the votes; on the second ballot, more than two-thirds, with a good margin. It was a solemn time for me. My inner struggle to know and to do the will of God was intense. I really wanted the pastoral ministry and was enjoying my work to a superlative degree. Besides, I did not know how I could leave my family for the prolonged absences the position of general superintendent would require. Joe was 14; Maylou, 11; and John, 2 years of age. I recall that one morning after I had awakened but was still in bed, John came into the room, climbed up and sat down on my chest, and as I hugged the little fellow I thought, 'I can't do it!' But deep in my soul there was another voice speaking, and it seemed to me the situation in the church almost placed me under compulsion to heed the call of the district superintendents.

"The ballots were sealed, naturally. But my good friend, General Secretary S. T. Ludwig, unofficially kept me informed of the results. Dr. Chapman came back to Kansas City a few days afterward and spent the weekend, which happened to be at Easter time. Saturday he called me and said, 'I want to see you. Would you rather see me today or wait until Monday?' Without hesitation I said, 'Please, let's wait until Monday.' He agreed.

"When he met me on Monday morning, he informed me that I had been elected a general superintendent. He observed my response and said, 'You act like you already know.' I said, 'Well, Dr. Chapman, here in Kansas City it is hard to keep secrets, even if they are official.' I then told him I would accept the election, depending fully upon God's help.

"Dr. Chapman planned for an induction service in the upstairs of the old mansion at 2940 Troost where seminary chapels were held and in the building where general offices were located at that time. There, in the limited area of the third floor, friends gathered for the induction of a new, green general superintendent. Dr. Chapman conducted a very impressive ceremony." [A copy follows.]

# INDUCTION SERVICE
## for General Superintendent Williamson
## by James B. Chapman

Here in the presence of God and the angels, we have met for a little time of prayer and ceremony in initiating into the highest office in the reaches of the church, a man greatly beloved by us and trusted by our people everywhere. We have come here this day acknowledging that we build our house in vain except that God build it, and realizing that even though chosen by the vote of the people this man can be as colorless as Mathias, but for that divine sanction that would make a Paul of Tarsus out of him. We have here representatives from every department of the church—officials and administrators, educators and editors, ministers and laymen. We are here to renew our vows of fidelity to God and to the Church of the Nazarene, and to avow our sanction of our newly elected leader. We are here to bestow upon him our blessings and promised cooperation.

Will Dr. Jarrette Aycock please stand as representing the district superintendents of the church; Rev. Fletcher Spruce, the pastors; Dr. Hugh C. Benner, the seminary; Brother M. Lunn, the Nazarene Publishing House; Dr. T. W. Willingham, the radio league; Miss Emma Word, the women's missionary society and our foreign missionary enterprise; Dr. Albert Harper, the Department of Church Schools; Mrs. Dorothy Davidson, the Nazarene Young People's Society; Brother John Stockton, the material and stewardship phases of the work; Dr. Corlett, the *Herald of Holiness,* and Dr. S. T. Ludwig, representing, as he does as general church secretary, the whole recorded membership and strength of our people. I stand here as representative of the Board of General Superintendents.

Now, Dr. and Mrs. Williamson, please come forward and stand facing this group. Beloved brother and sister, these from the various offices that stand here before you represent our church. I stand here today not only personally, but representing our 200,000 Nazarenes, our members in this country and around the world, to bid you Godspeed and promise you our prayers, our cooperation, and to tell you that you can count on us and the people we represent to sustain and support you in the great responsibility this task involves. You can count on us to pray for you and to hold you in continual remembrance before the Father's throne as you lead on in establishing the work of holiness in the hearts and minds of men. You can count on us to follow your leadership, even as we are assured you will endeavor to follow Christ.

Dr. Williamson, we welcome you as our general superintendent, and we thank God for you. We believe that like one of old, you have come to the kingdom for such a time as this. We welcome you in the name of the Father who brought you, in the name of the Christ who bought you, and in the name of the ever-blessed Holy Spirit who sought you. And may God grant you strength and wisdom to lead this so needy a people for many years to come.

And now let us gather about for prayer. The general superintendency is not an order but an office. The order is the elder. But it is an office involving so many of the characteristics of an order until I feel if we would pray for God to put His hand upon Dr. Williamson, it would be most appropriate.

O God, this man's name is Gideon. The Midianites were not more real than are the enemies of the church and God today. The times call for men of courage as leaders, and for men and women of courage as followers. May this Gideon lead while we break our pitchers, blow our trumpets, wave our torches, and win the victory for God and souls.

And now, Lord God, we come today with thanksgiving and with prayer. We present Brother and Sister Williamson before Thee. Look Thou in tender mercy upon this Thy servant and upon Thine handmaïden, and be gracious unto them. Lay Thy hand upon them in love and in blessing. May they be strong and of good courage. We ask that Thou wilt bless Sister Williamson in the added responsibility that will come to her. And wilt Thou come on Brother Williamson in a new way. We don't know any way to make the burden lighter except to make the man stronger. But, God, Thou canst make him so strong, the yoke will be easy. As we place our hands upon his head, wilt Thou place Thy hands anew upon his heart and may the days to come in his life and the life of the church be great because of grace and because of glory.

And now, let us pray as our blessed Lord taught us, "Our Father which art in heaven, Hallowed be thy name. Thy kingdom come, Thy will be done in earth, as it is in heaven. Give us this day our daily bread. And forgive us our debts as we forgive our debtors. And lead us not into temptation, but deliver us from evil: For thine is the kingdom, and the power, and the glory, for ever. Amen."

I, Audrey, want to break in at this point with a personal word. When rumor had it that Gideon's name was prominent in the balloting, I went to prayer. I did not see how I could rear the children with their father gone most of the time. I had had nine years of it at ENC, and I felt I could not take it again.

The only verse God gave me as I prayed was, "As a prince hast thou power with God and with men, and hast prevailed" (Gen. 32:28), and that wasn't the one I wanted.

I dressed and went to the induction ceremony. Bob and Glaphre Harding and Ray and Edith Moore were on the staff at First Church. They pinned a big orchid on my suit jacket. I thanked them but felt like saying, "Sorry, kids, but you know I can't go through with this."

But I kneeled beside my husband and heard Dr. Chapman say, "This man's name is Gideon and even as the Midianites were arrayed against the Israelites, so the forces of sin and evil are arrayed against the forces of righteousness today. Help us to follow this modern Gideon and to break our pitchers and hold up our torches." And just then something happened to me! I felt the enabling power of God possess me! And I knew I could do whatever I had to do! In the 22 years my Gideon served the church as a general superintendent, I bade him good-bye hundreds of times and I spent hundreds of days away from him. But I don't believe he ever saw me shed a tear nor heard me offer a word of complaint. I shed plenty of tears and I had to pray countless times for grace and wisdom. But God's visitation to me that morning was verified and renewed time after time. He did enable me to do what I had to do.

And now to continue G. B.'s narrative:

"Developments in the Board of General Superintendents came rapidly thereafter. Dr. John W. Goodwin, emeritus, had died in January of 1945, and Dr. Williams in March of 1946. Dr. Chapman, with whom I served for about 15 months, died in late July of 1947. That meant the superintendency was left with Dr. Miller, who had only seven years' experience; Dr. Powers, who had three years' experience; and I, who had one year. Since we were in the last year of the quadrennium, it was decided that we would not call for an election by the district superintendents since one had already been elected by that process in the quadrennium.

"The General Assembly of 1948 recommended the election of five general superintendents. The incumbents, Miller and Powers, were elected and I, also, was elected for the first time by the General Assembly. Then Dr. O. J. Nease was elected. Next in the running was Dr. Hugh C. Benner. There were those who felt strongly that he should continue as president of the seminary. He did not receive the required two-thirds of the ballots. The name of Dr. Samuel Young came into prominence and he was elected.

"About six months later, in December 1948, Dr. Miller died of a heart attack. An election was called during the January meeting of the district superintendents in Kansas City, and Dr. D. I. Vanderpool was elected. This board served until 1952, when Dr. Benner was elected a general superintendent. That board served together for eight years until 1960, when a sixth superintendent was ordered and Dr. V. H. Lewis was added to the board.

"The *Manual* of the Church of the Nazarene had from the beginning set forth very high standards for the conduct and deportment of its members. Certain 'worldly' practices were specifically prohibited. But in the quadrennium of 1948-52, a strong segment of the church began to gather around men who were making their own extralegal interpretations of what the Bible and the *Manual* designated as 'worldliness.' Their attacks were principally against the wearing of wedding bands and the use of television. The implications were that their opinions were the standards of the church; that the church had traditionally and historically taken a stand against the wearing of wedding bands as worldly adornment; and that though television was recognized as a potential instrument for the promotion of good, it could also be used for the promotion of evil. The real issue was whether a person who had strong biblical convictions should own a TV and be selective in its use, or whether the church should take a stand against television as an evil and make a rule that a television set could not be possessed by members of the church.

"The general superintendents as a board felt that it was not the time for them to come out with a declaration of principles and chose to remain silent. I had the conviction that I should speak my own mind on the subject. I realized that it would bring opposition from certain quarters. But I wrote some articles that were published in the *Herald of Holiness.* One was on 'The Errors of Eccentric Emphasis'; another was on the historic position of the church regarding the wedding band. I stated the ruling of the Board of General Superintendents made in the quadrennium 1940-44, made before any of the present board was in office, to the effect that plain wedding bands were not to be included in the prohibition of the church against worldly adornment.

"I also wrote another article in which I quoted the general rules and defended their scriptural basis. I took the position that if we began adding to the rules, this would eventually be the inspiration for subtracting from the rules. I believe they are a sacred heritage from our fathers and we should keep them as such.

"These articles caused quite a little commotion, especially

in certain quarters where the legalistic views had been defended vigorously. I realized that I was inviting the negative votes of a segment of the General Assembly. I allowed that I would possibly get as many as 100 negatives. I was told by some that I might get as many as 150. I went to the General Assembly calm and confident in my own spirit. I told the other members of the board that if I was elected by one vote, I would serve; and if I was not elected, that it would be all right. The night before the election, I slept peacefully and was awakened by my telephone wake-up call to rise and go about the duties of the day. I learned that at least two of my colleagues had spent the night in a cold sweat because of their concern about what would happen in the election.

"When the ballot was taken and reported, Dr. Ed Mann, who was on one board of tellers, brought me the report. He quoted from Ps. 17:5, 'The hills melted,' and let me know that my election was safe but that I had lost 72 votes. When I accepted the election, I said, 'The will of the Lord be done. I shall continue to exercise myself to have a conscience void of offense toward God and toward men. I promise to serve you to the best of my ability "With charity for all and malice toward none."'

"Of course, there was some uneasiness among those who believed that I had taken a liberal view and defended it. But as a matter of fact, I felt a certain freedom of leadership after that General Assembly. Soon after, I was preaching in a prominent church. Mrs. R. T. Williams was present and said to me, 'You are preaching with new freedom. You have had your baptism of fire.' Dr. Williams had said to me shortly before his death, 'If we ever have a division in the Church of the Nazarene, it will be over a question of legalism.' I remembered that, and I made up my mind to take my stand.

"With me were the leaders of the church who really represented the true spirit of the church, desiring to maintain the standards of other-worldliness and at the same time avoid the pitfalls of legalism. I had comfort in the words of E. O. Chalfant. In his characteristic way, he said, 'You did your duty! You did your duty! You did your duty!' L. T. Wells, longtime superintendent of the Kentucky District, said, 'We didn't know what position to take, but you showed us the way.'

"My concept of the office of a general superintendent was that he had very little power and should not try to exercise power, but that he did possess great influence and should be faithful in exercising that influence according to his God-given convictions. Some folks thought my action was unnecessary. But I believe time has proved that what I did, though I did it on my own, was better than had the Board of General Superintendents spoken out in defense of the things for which I stood. Then the entire board might have come under criticism. I took the stigma upon myself voluntarily and survived the General Assembly. I never was high man in the elections, but I did enjoy a sense of independence and freedom in offering leadership according to my convictions. I was always loyal to the expressed rulings of the board, but where they did not commit themselves, I felt not only free but duty-bound to offer leadership according to the light God gave me."

Now may I, Audrey, interrupt Gideon's narrative with a quote from Cameron Hawley. He writes:

> More and more, men are yielding to some terrible compulsion to conform, to think alike, and talk alike—yes, even to look alike. A man finds happiness only by walking his own path across the earth, thinking with his own mind, standing on his own two feet.

Gideon Williamson had to walk his own path. Neil B. Wiseman, pastor, Pompano Beach, Fla., said of him under date of December 31, 1981:

> He gave meaning to an assignment or role by who he was. Some men are shaped by responsibility, election, or power. But G. B. Williamson infused all of these with his faith, his character, his convictions. He was G. B. Wil-

liamson a long time before he was G. B. Williamson the pastor, the educator, or the general superintendent.

He more than filled those assignments with courageous competence. Integrity, love, and unquestioned commitment to the cause of holy living was the name of his game. Everywhere he went, he preached. And since he believed the Bible contained the answer to human needs, his pulpit work centered on applying the message of the Word of God to ecclesiastical and individual life. I believe the Church of the Nazarene stands bigger in spirit and size because Gideon Brooks Williamson lived and led.

No other one person has so shaped my ministry, inspired me to courageous service, affirmed my unique gifts, and believed in me more.

The decades that follow these events just recorded were deeply significant in the history of the Church of the Nazarene. It was a period of stabilization and growth. We were putting down our roots and were becoming recognized as a permanent institution among the many and varied church denominations. The Nazarene church was never a "sect," though it had been dubbed as such. As we matured and strengthened, that image was replaced by a growing awareness and respect for the position we were assuming among religious bodies.

The Board of General Superintendents of this era was composed of strong and devoted men. They were "middle of the roaders." They had a vision and a spirit of adventure, but they were aware of the pitfalls on either side of the Highway of Holiness that our founding fathers had committed us to follow. They were dedicated to the *Manual* of the Church of the Nazarene. I can remember my husband saying to gatherings of preachers upon occasion, "You have two little black books, your Bible and the *Manual*. You are to follow both."

It was at this time that he determined in one year to emphasize in all of his assemblies the guidelines laid down in the *Manual* for church membership, primarily upon the positive aspects of our creed. He pled for perfect love to be demonstrated, first toward God, then toward all the members of the Body of Christ. He urged our people to be busy in seeking out the unsaved and pressing upon them the claims of the gospel. He pressed upon his hearers their responsibility to the poor and needy. He urged faithful attendance at all the means of grace and also conscientious tithing. With characteristic vigor he attacked quarreling, gossiping, and the spreading of rumors.

He challenged pastors to preach upon these standards, all of which have scriptural basis. Thus, they would be lifting the tone and the quality of the laity of the local churches and emphasizing the principles for which the Church of the Nazarene stands.

A retired missionary reported recently that at this time, he was laboring in a field where legalism had seriously divided the people. He asked Gideon to repeat his messages on the *Manual* when he visited the field, with the result that many of the problems were solved. This occurred on more than one mission assignment.

In this emphasis, Gideon did not stand alone. His colleagues on the board were united in their purpose to guard the foundations of our doctrines and to encourage high living and sound ethical practice on the part of our members.

Progress was made in this era in strengthening the institutions of the church. The various departments represented at headquarters enjoyed stabilization, recognition, and outreach. Among them were the Nazarene Publishing House with its added spectrum of publications; the Department of Church Schools and Christian Life; the Nazarene Young People's Society; the Departments of Home and World missions; the Department of Evangelism; and the Department of Pensions and Benevolence. They were manned by able leaders and a loyal staff. A structured communications department for the church became a growing concern. Education as represented by our seminary and our colleges was put upon a stable and reliable basis of operation.

As the church grew and districts were divided and new ones were formed, growing recognition was given to the importance and stature of our district superintendents. Their qualifications for the office became a growing consideration.

New attention was given to the children and youth of the church. Organized activities were formed and given high priority and received enthusiastic response. Among them were the caravan programs, student mission corps, vacation Bible schools, and teenage societies and incentives.

All of this was stimulated by the need for expansion of interests, and the awareness of social and cultural developments outside the church, that we might remain current and serve the present age. But it was also characterized by a strong desire on the part of the Board of General Superintendents to "see and ask for the old paths, where is the good way, and walk therein." A new generation of Nazarenes was being incorporated into the life of the church. Some of them were from old-line denominations, persons who had become disillusioned with their former church relationships and had turned to the more vital and aggressive spirit of the Church of the Nazarene. They needed not only to be involved in the program, but also to be established in the doctrine and beliefs of the church. As always in an evangelical body, some were coming into the church without any religious background and, after being converted, needed to be instructed and established in the faith.

But there was another group for which there was a deep concern. They were the second-generation Nazarenes who had grown up in the church and had accepted its emphasis and procedures without these things ever becoming a personal conviction. It was disturbing to think that we might merely assume their loyalty without ever bringing them to the point of a deep personal commitment. For that reason, it was maintained that a strong doctrinal and evangelistic emphasis should be continually preserved in every local church to assure its fidelity to the entire denomination. Constant alertness at this point would care for the inevitable turnover that characterizes any growing religious body.

There was no thought on the part of Gideon Williamson that he and his contemporaries were the final word or that "wisdom would die with them," as Job tauntingly reminded his accusers. They had come to the kingdom for such a time as this, but when their day was done, they desired to pass the torch to a host of eager and dedicated followers. Gideon believed in the ongoing of the Church of Jesus Christ and in that segment of the body represented by the Church of the Nazarene. His confidence was positive and strong in the ultimate triumph of the church. He was deeply concerned for its leadership. But with Carl Sandburg, he could proclaim, and did to his final days, his confidence that,

> The strong men keep coming on!
> Call hallelujah, call amen; call deep thanks,
> The strong men keep coming on.

# FOREIGN VISITATION

Audrey: You began foreign visitation soon after your election to the general superintendency, didn't you?

Gideon: Yes, in 1947. My first assignment was to the Republic of Mexico. And I arranged for Dr. H. T. Reza to go with me as my interpreter. This was a most fortunate thing for me. He was an excellent interpreter and there were times when the tide of blessing rose high and people were rejoicing even while the Word was being preached. I especially remember preaching on being filled with the Spirit while people wept and praised God for the fact that Pentecost is available in the church today.

Audrey: Did you know what to do in Mexico?

Gideon: Well, before I left on the trip, Dr. Chapman told me, "Your ignorance is your greatest asset." So I felt well qualified! I knew there were personality problems. Some of the charges being made were not well founded and certainly not proved. After visiting the Central and Southeast districts, I proposed uniting them into one district for the time being under the leadership of David Sol. There was some reluctance, but the plan was adopted and eased some of the tensions.

Audrey: Wasn't the Southeast District Assembly held in Arriaga? And wasn't there a funny story about that?

Gideon: Oh, yes. This is where Dr. Reza had many friends. After preaching one night, he was detained visiting and I decided to go on alone to the hotel. It was a few blocks away. The streets were rather dark, and as I walked along, I saw a man coming toward me. Before we met, he turned and backed up aginst the wall and waited while I passed. I went on a little farther and heard heavy footfalls running to catch up with me. Thinking it might be the man I had just met, I quickened my pace and got to the gate of the enclosure wherein the hotel was located and found it locked. With a firm hand and with great vigor, I laid hold on the little knocker on the gate and it came off in my hand. It was purely decorative! Realizing that there was nothing I could do but await what might happen, I turned my back to the wall and looked in the direction of the approaching figure. Out of the shadows emerged Dr. Reza, to my great relief. He did warn me not to leave alone again. And you can be sure I did take his advice seriously.

Audrey: How long did you keep jurisdiction in Mexico?

Gideon: About six years. The church had been sending a different superintendent every year. I felt it would have a stabilizing effect to have continuity in leadership for a period of time, especially since Mexico did not allow us to send in any missionary personnel. This proved to be true. Difficulties disappeared and the church began to grow. In 1952, I went with Dr. Benner and turned jurisdiction over to him. The Department of World Missions established the Department of Spanish Publications and made Dr. Reza head of the department. His leadership in that field has been, in large measure, responsible for the gratifying growth that has characterized the more recent years. Soon thereafter, I was also assigned a visit to Peru, Nicaragua, and Guatemala.

Audrey: I remember on your return you said, "Peru is dark, dark, dark!"

Gideon: There were some deep problems. I am glad to say the Peruvian district in more recent years has made substantial progress and was one of the first to become a regular district.

Audrey: Tell me about Nicaragua.

Gideon: In San Jorge, I visited Dr. David Ramiros. In his early days, he had been a leader in Nicaraguan affairs. He had gone to Chicago to study, and while there lost his spiritual experience and even denied his faith. But he did attend Chicago First Church while H. V. Miller was pastor, got under conviction, and got back to the Lord and returned to Nicaragua to preach the gospel to his people. When Dr. Miller later visited the field as a general superintendent, he said he found the influence of Dr. Ramiros like "a handful of corn on the top of the mountain."

When I visited David Ramiros, he was blind and bedfast. He reached his bony arms up under the mosquito netting canopy and said, "Brother Williamson, I claim a Bible school for Nicaragua." I promised him I would do my best. After I got back home, I was given permission to raise a special. The Northern California District, under Roy Smee, pledged $13,000 to start a Bible college in Nicaragua. A valuable piece of land that bordered on Lake Nicaragua became available. It was purchased and appropriate buildings were erected. The school operated for many years under missionary leadership with the help of nationals. I believe it justified its existence.

Audrey: I remember yet the names of some of the missionaries who were on the field then. We prayed for them so often in our home.

Gideon: Yes, yes. The Harold Stanfields, the C. T. Rudeen family, Cora Walker, Esther Crain. They were a heroic band. From there I went on to Guatemala. Here I became acquainted with Robert and Pearl Ingram, veterans who had served with the founder of the mission, R. S. Anderson and his wife. Their strong leadership was beginning to bear fruit. I wrote their story in the missionary reading book *Sent Forth by the Holy Ghost.* I also established a warm personal relationship with the Russell Birchards, Mrs. Birchard being the daughter of the R. S. Andersons.

Audrey: Wasn't it on this visit you met William Sedat?

Gideon: Yes, he was engaged in translating the New Testament into the Kekchi language. In a conference in Kansas City some time later, he presented me a copy of this finished work which I have prized highly. He spent probably 14 to 16 years in completing this monumental task.

Audrey: The Latin people laid hold of you very deeply on this trip, didn't they? Weren't you gone about nine weeks?

Gideon: I believe so. I remember that afterward when I met the Board of General Superintendents, I told them that if they would assign me Latin America for life or as long as I was a general superintendent, I would learn the Spanish language and take responsibility for that area of our mission work. They did not accept my proposal.

Audrey: But you did visit other Latin countries in the course of the years.

Gideon: Yes, I made the exploratory trip to Brazil in 1958 and suggested we establish our center in Campinas, where we would have a Bible school, and that we should also look forward to Bello Horizonte in the state of Minas Geras for a venture into more virgin territory.

Audrey: I wanted so desperately to go with you on that trip to Brazil, but I didn't see how I could be spared at home nor how we could afford it. I was praying about it and asked God to give me some indication of His will. The *Kansas City Times* published a Bible verse every day, and I eagerly opened the paper one morning believing it would show me God's will. It did. The verse for the day was, "Why gaddest

97

thou about so much to change thy way?" (Jer. 2:36). I dropped the subject!

Gideon: Yes, but you did get to go with me in 1971, after I was out of office, and we went on our own unofficially.

Audrey: Yes, and how grateful I am for that trip: Mexico, Guatemala, Nicaragua, Costa Rica, Panama, Colombia, Peru; and across the Andes to Argentina, Brazil, Uruguay; then Venezuela, Trinidad, Tobago, Puerto Rico, Haiti, and Jamaica. What a precious memory! It was all "exceeding abundantly"! Afterward we wrote the missionary reading book *Then and Now.*

Gideon: I had made several trips to Argentina prior to that last visit. John Cochran and his wife had gone out in 1936 and had vision and faith for a strong and growing church. John Cochran's outlook was like Abraham's when God said, "Look east, west, north, and south. All that you can see, I'll give you." His vision was and is being fulfilled even into Uruguay, Chile, and Brazil.

Audrey: We had our world trip in 1950-51.

Gideon: I offered to make a trip to visit several fields and thus save travel expense. By this time, the General Board had voted to allow general superintendents to take their wives with them on one foreign trip each quadrennium. We left San Francisco in October and sailed for Honolulu, Hawaii, on the famous passenger ship the Lurline.

Audrey: Excuse me, but a storm arose before we were out of sight of the Golden Gate Bridge, and I was seasick most of the way to the Islands. But go on—

Gideon: We held an assembly in Honolulu with Leo Baldwin as superintendent, visited several of the other islands, and explored the possibility of opening work in Hilo. Then we set sail for Australia on the old Aorangi.

Audrey: What a marvelous trip as we sailed "down under" and the Southern Cross appeared above us at night.

Gideon: We stopped at Auckland, New Zealand, remember, and went out to Rotorura where I found the grave of my great uncle, Seymour Mills Spencer, who had gone out as a missionary to the Maori tribe in 1854. He never returned to the United States but lived and died in New Zealand.

Audrey: I will never forget when you found that grave. I had lingered in the Maori temple across the way, and I heard your voice ring out, "Seymour Mills Spencer was my father's uncle," and 200 tourists who were around the place came running.

Gideon: A story never loses anything when you tell it, for sure! But I did write an article for the *Herald of Holiness* in which I told of the possibilities in New Zealand. Brother Rollie Griffith read the article and proposed to go to New Zealand to open the work there. He was told no financial support would be available, but he decided to go anyway and finance his own venture. The beginning of the work in New Zealand came as a result of my first stop there and later Brother Griffith's work was taken over by the General Board.

Audrey: From there we went to Australia where we spent six weeks.

Gideon: Yes, I felt it important to spend some time there because American leadership had found it difficult to continue, and the work in its early stages had been turned over to the Australian superintendent, A. A. E. Berg. We enjoyed the Australian people very much. I preached in most of the churches, conducted an assembly, and ordained some ministers.

Audrey: We spent Christmas there. Howard Hamlin had given us a money gift to spend somewhere on our trip, and with it we took the Bergs to Christmas dinner at the Lennons Hotel. This had been General McArthur's headquarters during World War II, so a lot of American influence remained. It was 102 degrees outside, but in air-conditioned comfort we had a marvelous traditional Christmas dinner. An entertainer moved from table to table, singing request numbers. When he came to our table, I tried to ask for "I'm Dreaming of a White Christmas," but burst into tears as soon as the words were out. I missed the children so desperately. But it was a happy occasion anyway. I have always been grateful to Howard and Maxine.

Gideon: From Adelaide, Australia, we sailed to Bombay, India, with a brief stopover in Ceylon.

Audrey: By some good fortune, we were seated at the captain's table on that voyage. One morning at breakfast, he seemed unusually weary. I asked him why. I never forgot his reply. "These waters can be treacherous. I spent the night on the bridge so you would sleep soundly."

Gideon: Those were troubled days, too, in the world picture. It was comforting to remember that our Captain was on the bridge. I arrived in India, the first general superintendent to visit that field since World War II.

Audrey: Yes, the missionaries were so hungry for fellowship: the Bealses, the Leslie Fritzlans, Earl and Hazel Lee, Dr. Witthoff, Jean Darling, Geraldine Chappell, Miss Willox, the Greers. What a marvelous group they were!

Gideon: We went by train to Malkapur in the Central Provinces where our Nazarene mission had its base of operations. Missionaries from Buldana and Chikhli met us. An important Indian personality was on the train, and a brass band was out to welcome him. Brother Beals slipped around and as we got off, he asked them to play an American tune for us. It was "A Bicycle Built for Two." Very appropriate!

Audrey: Samuel Bhujbal was the Indian district superintendent. A fine man and a skillful interpreter.

Gideon: We had a most enjoyable visit. I held the district assembly which had some very inspiring services in connection with it, and I also preached in the jungle camp meeting, as it was called. It was held under a tent and large crowds heard the gospel. Estelle Crutcher, Hazel Lee's mother, was there and did some of the preaching. She was always God-anointed.

Audrey: We visited the excellent coeducational school in Chikhli which Orpha Cook had established, and also visited the hospital at Basim, now Washim. I spoke at the nurses' graduation ceremony, I remember.

Gideon: Yes. The work of education and of medical missions rightly follows a venture in a land of such vast need, where illiteracy is widespread and where attention to health and sanitation is so necessary. But we found the evangelistic thrust always in the vanguard of our work in India.

Audrey: We stayed four weeks in India. I recall so vividly our trip into Aurangabad where the gospel had not been preached. The missionaries arranged for a slide presentation on a large outdoor screen. They estimated perhaps 2,000 people came to see the pictures that depicted the life of Christ. They were seated on the ground. Twice there was a visible response; once when the picture of the baby Jesus in the manger was shown, and again when He hung upon the Cross. It was as though a breeze moved across a field of ripened grain. The Advent and the Crucifixion; Bethlehem and Calvary! They are the heart of the gospel.

Gideon: Yes, I have often prayed that light might come to those darkened souls. From India, we again took ship and sailed across the Indian Ocean through the Suez Canal to disembark at Port Said, Egypt, and then by motorcar to Cairo.

Audrey: We wrote "Jesu, Masiki Jay" ("Victory to Jesus") on that voyage, the story of our days in India.

Gideon: That's right. After a few days in Egypt, viewing some of the impressive sights of that ancient land, we flew to Beirut, Lebanon. Our work was new at that time in that part of the world.

Audrey: Yes, I recall the progress that had been made when we had our return trip in 1967. The Bible college and day school in Beirut had been built and were flourishing in that beautiful building two stories on the land side, six stories on the sea side, facing out to the blue Mediterranean. The American influence was strong and positive with the great American university in Beirut.

Gideon: What a sad contrast to the present state of affairs in Lebanon! But seed sown is never lost. From Lebanon we went to Jordan. In 1967, Berge and Doris Najarian were our efficient hosts and guides. The work in Amman was progressing. We had several profitable services, and I baptized a class of members in the Jordan at the traditional site.

Audrey: Retracing the steps of Jesus in Jerusalem and the Holy Land was an awesome experience for me. The first time, in 1951, it was with our dear missionary Samuel Krikorian. I shall never forget praying under the old olive tree in Gethsemane where he and Dr. Reynolds had wrestled with God the night before permission was received for the Church of the Nazarene to enter the city of Jerusalem.

Gideon: Yes, and in 1967, Alex Wachtel was our most interesting guide as we drove north to Nazareth, visiting our splendid property there and circling the Lake of Galilee to visit Capernaum.

Audrey: I remember how pensive you became as you recalled Jesus' words, "And thou, Capernaum, which art exalted unto heaven, shall be brought down to hell: for if the mighty works, which have been done in thee, had been done in Sodom, it would have remained until this day."

Gideon: We had a meal of bread and fish beside the Sea of Galilee, a sweet memory.

Audrey: Returning to Italy in 1967, we also saw much progress since our earlier trip in 1951.

Gideon: Yes, and the work in Germany had been opened in the interim. Jerry and Alice Johnson were making substantial gains, and the European Bible College had been established at Büsingen.

Audrey: Oh, that was a moving experience for me. I can hear John Nielson yet leading the students in singing "Surely Goodness and Mercy Shall Follow Me." Our Bible colleges throughout the world have certainly been significant in training national workers to become strong leaders in their respective lands.

Gideon: We ended our long trip in 1951 in the British Isles.

Audrey: Yes, you made a number of visits there and they have been profitable. You have loved the British people.

Gideon: Yes, I knew Dr. Sharpe and George Frame, both courageous leaders. I have visited England, Scotland, Ireland, and Wales, and have been especially concerned with the work in Wales under Frank Webster.

Audrey: You went to the Orient in 1953.

Gideon: Yes, I stopped in Hawaii where good progress was being made under Dr. Cecil Knippers. He followed Ansel Gunter there. Then I flew to New Zealand to see the work being done by Rollie Griffith. I preached in the garage of his home and saw a woman sanctified; two of her sons later entered the ministry of the Church of the Nazarene, one of them being ordained by Dr. Coulter some years later. Rollie Griffith was working hard with pick and shovel to lay the foundation for a church in volcanic rock. But he put his life into it, and the First Church of Auckland was organized. Across the years, the work has gained and is now moving ahead splendidly under the inspiration of Dwight and Evonne Neuenschwander.

I moved from there to Australia. Dr. Richard Taylor had gone there to be the founder and first president of the Australian Nazarene Bible College. A fine piece of property with adaptable buildings was located in the Sydney area. The NYPS in the United States had pledged to raise $25,000 to purchase property for the Bible college. But the money was not yet in. I called John Stockton to send the $25,000, which he did, with the approval of one or more available general superintendents. It was one of the greatest risks I ever took. But the deal was made, the money was forthcoming, and the Bible college functioned there for some years, serving both Australia and New Zealand. Later the property was sold and the Bible college moved to a location in the Brisbane area. I flew then to the Philippines.

Audrey: Yes, and I flew out and met you there. How exciting!

Gideon: I nearly broke my neck looking up at the overcast sky until the pilot of your plane found a crack in the clouds and brought you in for a safe landing.

Audrey: I enjoyed the days in the Philippines, especially the time spent at the Bible college in Baguio City. The Pattees were serving there then.

Gideon: We found some very loyal, capable missionaries and some promising national workers. From the Philippines we flew to Japan, where we spent more than two weeks. We were welcomed royally by Will Eckel, the Harrison Davises, the Hubert Hellings, the Merril Bennetts, and the other missionaries. Dr. Eckel had reopened the work after it had been shut down during World War II. The former leaders, notably Kitagawa and Isayama, responded to his leadership, and when we were there in 1953 there were a number of good and growing churches. Dr. Eckel understood the Japanese and had their viewpoint.

Audrey: I remember visiting the coeducational school at Chiba.

Gideon: Yes, when I returned home and gave my report to the General Board, I recommended that we take it over and make it a Nazarene training center. The assembly in Japan had voted to do this. But there was formidable opposition, and I had to send Dr. Eckel word that the decision was not favorable. However, in the next quadrennium, when Dr. Benner was on the field, he felt strongly that the Chiba project should be undertaken by the church, and the board was then ready to accept his recommendation with my support. The results have highly justified the decision.

Audrey: I guess you were looking a long way down the road.

Gideon: Be that as it may. I greatly enjoyed my visit to Japan. Ross Kida was my interpreter, and an excellent one. We had a great assembly and fine response in the churches visited.

Audrey: I know you never took advantage of a foreign trip just to see the sights of the country. If they were in line with your itinerary, then you were grateful. We did visit Osaka, Nara, and Hiroshima besides Tokyo. I guess that leaves Africa to round out the major trips you took, though many of them have not been mentioned.

Gideon: I went first to Africa in 1961. Son John was a high school senior and I took him with me and paid his way since you could not leave home at that time.

We spent ten and one-half weeks in the country, visiting all the areas where the church had work as well as the historic sites including Pigg's Peak, Endingeni, Manzini,

Stegi, Acornhoek with their schools, hospitals, and preaching points. It is a vast and thrilling undertaking.

I conducted the assembly and council meeting where 120 missionaries were present. It was unanimously voted to organize some mission districts and also to buy land adjacent to the European Bible College in Florida and establish a publishing house that would serve all areas and languages in our African field.

Perhaps the plan was too idealistic. It never did seem to get the practical cooperation of all areas and the blending of the human factors involved. Therefore, the project has since been canceled and the property turned over to the Bible college. Maybe there was a providence in it after all, for the publishing house property became a real addition to the Bible college and has been adapted to the administrative and teaching purposes of the school.

Dr. George Coulter was World Missions secretary at the time and was most cooperative in carrying out all my recommendations. The General Board, too, gave full endorsement to the plans I had made.

Following that visit, I wrote the missionary reading book *African Safari.*

Audrey: In two years, you made a second trip to Africa.

Gideon: Yes, remember I went alone and spent four weeks. Then you joined me and we spent an additional six weeks. Between visits, I had pledged $10,000 to build a new church in Johannesburg. Upon my return, the new church was practically completed and services and the assembly were held there. I also pledged money for a building in Bulawayo, Zambia, and a substantial sum was pledged for a church in Capetown. These churches are now a part of the European work in South Africa.

It so happened while I was pastor of Kansas City First Church, before becoming a general superintendent, a special was proposed to build an R. T. Williams Memorial church among the Europeans of South Africa, and First Church pledged $15,000, which was used to build the first building erected in the European district at Vandervale Park.

Audrey: Your visits to Africa made a strong impression upon you. You left part of your heart there.

Gideon: Well, I have continued to feel a deep interest in the work there. In these days of transition and tension, my prayer is that God will overrule all hindrances and bring to fulfillment the vision, the dreams, the hopes of veteran missionaries such as Harmon Schmelzenbach, C. S. Jenkins, Carl Mishke, and their wives and families; and of Louise Robinson Chapman, Fairy Chism, Ora Lovelace, Elizabeth Cole, Dorothy Davis Cook, Lorraine Schultz, and all the rest.

Audrey: I do know you considered Dr. Esselstyn a wise and capable leader, and his children now follow in his footsteps.

Gideon: Yes, and I am grateful to Dr. Strickland and his family. We spent more time in their home than anywhere else and had some very gratifying experiences.

Audrey: I have heard you tell how that at the close of your first visit, Mrs. Strickland served a lovely dinner and then passed the promise box. You drew the following lines:
> *Christ has sent me to the midnight lands,*
> *Mine be the ordination of the Pierced Hands.*

Gideon: All the noble band who have served Africa so faithfully and so well come before me. I would like to eulogize each one. Truly they have felt the ordination of the Pierced Hands. Many have given years of service until retirement brought them home. How rich their reward in heaven will be!

# NAZARENE BIBLE
# COLLEGE STORY

One summer, in order to strengthen our family life, the children and I traveled with Gideon as he presided in several assemblies. This was the way we managed a vacation. As we drove along the winding roads of Kentucky, we were playing the "Slopski" game. The first one to see a horse would call out "Slopski" and add one to his score. If we came upon a herd, pandemonium broke loose. Kentucky is a good place to play the game.

It seemed that Gideon was always the winner, even when he was driving. He was not only alert, he had far vision. On this particular day, he spotted two horses ahead on a hillside cropping grass. The road then dipped into a hollow, and the horses were hidden from view. Gideon said, "When we come up out of this valley, there will be two horses feeding on the opposite hill. I have seen them and they are both mine. Slopski! Slopski!"

The older children and I were skeptical; John, who was only five or six years of age, was totally credulous. And sure enough, when we began to climb the hill, there were the two "Slopskis." John's remark was unforgettable. He said, "Daddy can see a long way. He can even see around the bend in the road."

As I have contemplated and reviewed Gideon's gifts and abilities, I think I would say that his vision was his outstanding quality for leadership. He could see "a long way down the road," even sometimes "around the bend." This gift was recognized by many who looked to him for direction and guidance. But it was also the catalyst for most of the criticism and opposition he ever received in his promotion of an idea or a course of action. Fortunately, he lived long enough for much of that disagreement to be dispelled, as time and ensuing events proved he had not been off course after all. He did not like to stand virtually alone. He was not afraid to do so when he felt this was the price to be paid for true leadership. After he was gone, I found this quote from John R. Mott in my husband's file. I do not recall ever hearing him use it. I feel sure he never applied it to himself. But here it is : "Vision is to see what others do not see, to see farther than they see, and before they see."

It was in the late '50s when, home from an assignment, he walked into the kitchen where I was working and said, "How would you like to finish up at the Bible college?"

"What Bible college?" I asked.

"Nazarene Bible College," said he.

"I didn't know we had one," said I.

"We don't," said he.

"Well, if that's where you hope to be, I'd like it," I said, and that ended the conversation for the time being. But I had caught a glimpse of the vision he had seen down the road.

It was in the quadrennium of 1960-64 that the whole question of the adequacy of our training for ministers in the Church of the Nazarene was reviewed. As a matter of fact, in the General Assembly of 1960, a resolution had been presented for the establishment of a Bible college which received strong vocal support from such leaders as Dr. Howard Hamlin, Dr. Nicholas Hull, and Dr. Mark Moore. After some discussion, it was decided that the whole educational program of the church should be made a matter of study. Therefore, a commission of 21 knowledgeable persons—laymen, pastors, district superintendents, and leaders of our educational institutions—was established. They employed Dr. Leslie Parrott as research person. A grant from the Lily Foundation was secured, and at a cost of approximately $55,000, the field was surveyed. The commission was authorized to report to the General Board. Several times during the quadrennium, the Board of General Superintendents was consulted and recommendations were made. But the final report of the commission was not made to the General Board until January of 1964. It was a majority report recommending the establishment of two junior colleges and also recommending that the liberal arts colleges strengthen their Bible certificate courses to accommodate men who had responded late to the call of the ministry.

Since the General Assembly was only six months away, it was the action of both the Board of General Superintendents and the General Board that the commission report should go directly to the General Assembly without action of either board. This was done.

When the matter was presented to the General Assembly, there was serious opposition, especially from college institutional leaders, to the establishment of two junior colleges. This would mean adjustment of their zones and deprivation of some of their support in students and finances.

The recommendation that the liberal arts colleges strengthen their Bible certificate courses to accommodate persons whose education for the ministry had been delayed also was debated. A substitute motion was made which called for the elimination of this recommendation and called for the establishment of a Bible college in a central location in the quadrennium immediately following the General Assembly, the Board of Trustees to be nominated by the general superintendents and a nominating committee of the General Assembly and elected by the General Assembly. This Board of Trustees was to choose a location, elect a president upon recommendation of the general superintendents, and proceed with the establishment of a Bible college.

Strong and extended debate followed, in which the general superintendents participated as well as the delegates. When the secret ballot was finally taken and the report read, the General Assembly had ordered the establishment of a Bible college and two junior colleges.

We are in the fourth quadrennium since that historic action took place, and it is gratifying to note that all three of the institutions ordered by the General Assembly of 1964 have prospered. Mount Vernon Nazarene College at Mount Vernon, Ohio, and Mid-America Nazarene College at Olathe, Kans. are now both four-year, fully accredited liberal arts colleges. Nazarene Bible College, located at Colorado Springs, is accredited by the American Association of Bible Colleges. It has graduated 1,000 men and women, the most of whom are now in pastoral and evangelistic ministry.

Gideon had taken an active part in the debate that occurred in the General Assembly. In fact, he had left his seat on the platform with the general superintendents and had walked to a microphone on the floor of the assembly, had turned his back to the crowd, and had read the speech that here follows.

Mr. Chairman,

I have chosen to write what I have to say on this subject to make sure I express accurately what I think, and so that if I am quoted, I will not be misquoted. I ask that you listen attentively, observing the rules of debate, then I shall not be disheartened by absence of amens or by applause.

There is a compulsion upon me that I must speak to this subject. It could be in part due to the fact that I have had much to say over a period of 25 years about the need for a Nazarene Bible College. And now that the issue is drawn, I would feel less than consistent if I held my peace. But I am speaking primarily out of a deep conviction that there is now and will always be a need for a Bible college in the total educational structure of our church.

I have a deep concern lest the common defects of our natural eyesight may have their counterpart in our deeper insight to this important problem. We could be farsighted and therefore overlook some things that are in the picture of the immediate future. We could be nearsighted and therefore unable to see beyond the pressing problem of the institutions now in existence. We could be cross-eyed and see double, or we could have blind spots and in some areas see not at all. But our greatest danger is that we will have astigmatism, which results in an indistinct and fuzzy image on the brain. I hope that we shall not have hallucinations in which we see ghostly spectres to frighten us from the path of duty such as cost, location, or disturbance of the status quo or some opposition.

Before we reach a decision on this important question, it should be made perfectly clear that the need for a Bible college does not arise out of the failure of our college and seminary program. It rather stems from their outstanding success. They are doing a great work and will continue to do so. My own record of more than 40 years is one of unqualified support to these institutions. But my conviction that a Bible college is needed dates back to my own years as a college administrator. The colleges of liberal arts and the seminary must go on. Most of our leaders and a great percentage of our Christian workers will and should be trained on their campuses. Be it further understood that a Bible college must not be a center for legalism or fanaticism. It is not to encourage an attitude of super piety that it is needed. Neither is a Bible college needed to produce second-rate preachers. Of them we have now and always will have an oversupply, and no institution can be blamed and none can eliminate them.

What then are the reasons for a Bible college?

First. It will help and not hinder the colleges now functioning or that will function as the existing ones do! A Bible college will relieve the college administrators and staff of the necessity of offering Bible certificate courses or the equivalent thereof. These are, I am sure in the final analysis, a financial burden requiring added and separate instructors and buildings, and they can become a liability to the accreditation of the colleges. There is a constant demand for raising entrance requirements. It is beyond controversy that we have a responsibility to those of our youth who are not of college calibre and yet have useful lives before them and can render fruitful service.

Furthermore, the Bible college would provide some relief at the point of excessive enrollment, making the tremendous pressure for expansion less acute and keeping the enrollment of our colleges within the range of a small college with its decided advantages.

A Bible college, by filling a gap in our total educational program, will stimulate new enthusiasm and inspire new sacrifices for our educational institutions. This will result in greater liberality toward all the colleges and the seminary, and as Dr. H. C. Benner has often reminded us, there is enough money to support every Kingdom interest if we can tap the existing resources.

Second. A Bible college is needed to serve a segment of our youth and young adults that will not be reached by the present educational program. There are, according to our recently completed survey, 800 persons taking the home study course for ordination that are not enrolled in our colleges or seminary. One hundred twenty-six of these say they would enroll in a Nazarene Bible College if one were available. These do not include those enrolled in the course for local preachers. One hundred twenty-six more desire Bible certificate programs in existing institutions.

In addition, there is a group who are excluded because of the ever mounting cost of a college education even in the Church of the Nazarene. And these increases are justified and necessary.

In the great pool of potential students which is a cause of burden to Dr. Paul Updike, there are no doubt a few hundred who could not plan for a regular college of liberal arts education with possible graduate work who, I believe, would gladly respond to the open door of a Nazarene Bible College.

It is needed so that Bible certificate students can prepare in a setting in which they can feel they are among equals and not be inescapably, even if unintentionally, made to feel they are second-class passengers or senior citizens.

Third. The Nazarene Bible College is needed to fill a great and not a diminishing need in the ranks of the Nazarene ministry and Christian workers.

We cannot overlook the fact that more than 50 percent of Nazarene churches have no more than 50 members. College and seminary men do and will man some of these. Bible college men may prove capable of filling pulpits in larger churches and other places of leadership. Some with no more training have and do and may continue to do so. But if we keep our smaller churches supplied with pastors and organize a few thousand more in the next 25 years as we should, we will need the men of Bible college preparation. Our district superintendents see this and on the questionnaire sent to them voted as follows: Eight did not reply. Of those who did, 69 percent voted for a Bible college, while 31 percent voted against it for a variety of reasons, no doubt.

A Bible college will help us keep an active ministry that will hold our churches to the line of evangelical faith, vital experience of the new birth and entire sanctification. And they will be an anchor to windward for intense revival evangelism and all out for souls emphasis. This will be more needed 20 years from now than today.

My misgivings are not concerning our college leaders, but we are now at a time of decision as to the direction in which we will go. I hear more than whispers that some would favor a goal in the foreseeable future when all ordained ministers would be required to have as a minimum in formal education a regular college degree. I think we can learn from sister denominations. I would cite the two largest Protestant bodies of this nation. One has followed a course which, at least in theory, required college and seminary training for ordination. A recent official statement reveals that their seminaries are producing only one-half the required number of ministers to meet their need in replacements. They are short of preachers by thousands today, and they have fires of revival burning in only limited areas. They were once the greatest force for evangelism in America.

The other great and growing denomination has many Bible colleges. They have revivals far and wide and are growing faster than any major group in this country.

The United Church of Christ operates an undergraduate seminary for those without college degrees at Bangor, Me., to supply their need of preachers.

Which way shall we take?

It is a matter of record that one-half of all Protestant missionaries from North America are the product of Bible colleges. Which way do we take?

The information obtained by our recent study reveals that the percentage of ministerial graduates from our colleges and seminary has declined from 38 percent to 22 percent of the total number between 1956 and 1962. This could be explained on the basis of increased enrollment, but the total number has also decreased from 215 in 1956 to 158 in 1962.

What should the curriculum of the Bible college include? It should prepare men for ordination in not more than three years. It possibly and probably would also offer a four-year Bible course.

The Bible, The Book of books, should be the backbone of the curriculum. Preachers who know their Bible are not ignorant. Those who do not know it are poorly prepared to preach—whatever they know besides.

There should be thorough training in biblical theology. Preaching and practice should be given prominence. Use of the English language is basic. Public speaking should not be given a secondary emphasis. Churchmanship and church administration must be included. Religious education and church music should have their place. Missions and evangelism are among the musts.

The Church of the Nazarene needs one Bible college advantageously located for the maximum number. This proposed institution is needed as an integral part of our total educative program. It can be manned with able leaders. It can be financed without damage to existing institutions. It will help all of them to grow and it will serve in an area in which there is now a gap.

It should be ordered here and now and put in operation at the earliest possible date. If it is not done now, it probably will never be done officially.

There is extant a quotation from Dr. Chapman in which he pleaded for a college and seminary program. It is dated 40 years ago. We had no accredited colleges then and no seminary. The scene has changed. Furthermore, I am witness and others here are, too, that in the middle '40s, not long before his translation, Dr. Chapman endorsed and lent his support to the proposal of a Bible college so conceived and so dedicated. Had plans then proposed not been interrupted by legal proceedings, such an institution would have been in operation for the last 18 years.

Delegates of this Sixteenth General Assembly, I have unburdened my heart to you on this subject. The decision is your responsibility. By your vote I will be governed. But I believe you will hear my appeal, or 25 years from now many will wish you had. I plead for fair and prayerful consideration and for action in concern for the long-run results.

—G. B. WILLIAMSON

In taking this position favoring the Bible college, Gideon stood alone among the Board of General Superintendents. All of them opposed the establishment of the Bible college, and all of them opposed him for promoting it. This was not easy to take. But he had done what he felt compelled to do, and in so doing, he had not gone contrary to any action that had been taken by the board, for none had been taken.

This was the third time when "my men" prevented me from being with my husband at a time when he needed my presence. My father, who made his home with us and who was 96 years of age and totally blind, had just taken to his bed, not to get up again. He had never gone to bed in his life except at night to sleep, and he was convinced that he would not live long, though God did give him six more good years. But I could not leave him.

I did not know all that those days in the assembly would hold for Gideon. But I did know the pressures would be great. I literally spent my days and my nights in prayer for him. It was at that time that God quickened to me again the promise He had given me at the time of Gideon's election to the superintendency, "As a prince hast thou power with God and with men, and hast prevailed" (Gen. 32:28).

Gideon had high regard for the members of the Board of General Superintendents with whom he served till his termination. They were strong men and effective leaders. Differences of opinion and of procedure among them never resulted in a break in fellowship. They preserved a spirit of Christian love and personal esteem that was never sacrificed. Among other factors that contributed to this was a sense of humor that flashed out in potentially tense situations. The following true

117

story illustrates the fact that these men could laugh at and with each other.

As they were planning for the 1968 General Assembly, Dr. B. Edgar Johnson, general church secretary, came to the board. Their conversation follows:

*Johnson:* "How many microphones do you think we'll need on the floor of the General Assembly?"

*Williamson:* "How many did we have in 1964?"

*Johnson:* "Four, I believe."

*Williamson:* "Well, wasn't that about right?"

*Coulter:* "We had one too many in Portland."

*Williamson:* "Oh, you musn't muzzle the ox that treadeth out the corn."

*Young:* "What about the ass?"

*Williamson:* "Oh, he spake with a man's voice and rebuked the madness of the prophet."

That closed the discussion.

The general superintendents were reluctant to act in implementing the orders of the General Assembly, but in January of 1965, they did come to grips with the establishment of the Bible college. They nominated Dr. Charles H. Strickland for president, Gideon having voted for him on the first ballot. He was accepted by the Board of Trustees and at his post in Africa he was notified by cable of his election. He accepted. Thus he became the founding president of Nazarene Bible College.

Dr. Strickland tells this story on himself, and with his permission I repeat it. He was a delegate to the 1964 General Assembly, home from Africa for the event. As he left the session when the Bible college was ordered, he said to his wife, "Fannie, I didn't know how to vote, but I felt so sorry for old Doc Williamson, I voted yes. But God pity the nut they make president."

It is worthy of note that when the church called, Dr. Strickland responded. He knew full well that he was setting a new course. He was sailing an uncharted sea. But courageously and without hesitation, he tackled the job with energy, wisdom, and vision. He led effectively in the choice of the site at Colorado Springs, and with the able assistance of Dr. Cecil Ewell, proceeded to erect three buildings. Among the local men who were especially helpful in obtaining the location and in construction of the buildings were Bud Isham, layman, and pastors Dwight Neuenschwander of Trinity, Bill Sullivan of First Church, and Robert Leffel of Southgate.

Dr. Strickland chose well for his beginning faculty. Dr. Norman Oke was academic dean and head of the Department of Theology, and Professor Milo Arnold came as professor of practics after a long and admirable record as a pastor. Rev. Leffel was also on the faculty in its beginning days, moving from part-time to full-time relationship.

Anticipating Gideon's retirement from the general superintendency in 1968, we offered to go to the Bible college and serve on the faculty without salary. Our only intention was to be helpful to the president and the administration, and to use our influence, our experience, and our means to promote the cause to which he had given his vocal support. Our offer was accepted and we remained in this relationship for 12 years, Gideon in teaching of the Bible and I in communications.

These years at the Bible college were probably the most rewarding of all the years of our married life. We were together doing work that thrilled us both. Every day was an adventure. They were long days, for we taught both morning and evening classes. But we were given strength as our day. I believe Gideon felt these years were the climax of his service to the church. He was absorbed with his students' progress—teaching, inspiring, shepherding them. If one missed more than a class or two, he looked him up at home or at work or in the hospital. He challenged his students with his love of the Word and with his concept of the primacy of preaching. For several years he was college chaplain, and in this office he had prime opportunity to serve as guide and counselor. His ideal for Nazarene Bible College was that here men and women whose preparation for the Christian ministry had been delayed or inadequate should receive quality education of the highest calibre.

Scores of tributes from Nazarene Bible College alumni were received at the time of his Homegoing. Here are a few examples:

> There is no single other person who has given me more of an appreciation for the holiness message, the heritage of our church, or the quality of our leadership than Dr. Williamson.

> There is a new generation of men within our church who have experienced the realities of perfect love and are devoted to preaching it! There are a number of us who have been strongly affected by the legacy of Bresee and Reynolds and Williams and Chapman . . . and Williamson. Their experience and example evoke like response in us: a humble devotion to a holy God; consecrated acceptance of the Great Commission of our Lord Jesus Christ; obedience to and reliance upon the Holy Spirit; utter faith in the Word of God; a compelling compassion for the souls of men . . . and an undespairing loyalty to the Church of the Nazarene.
>
> Archie R. Hoffpauir, *Pastor*
> Waco First Church of the Nazarene
> NBC Graduate

> Written on the back page of the Bible I used while a student at NBC are these lines: Acts 20:24 (4/15/76, NBC): Dr. Williamson said today, "If any of you are called upon to preach my funeral, you may use this as your text, 'But none of these things move me, neither count I my life dear unto myself, so that I might finish my course with joy, and the ministry, which I have received of the Lord Jesus, to testify the gospel of the grace of God.'"

> Together you have both made a major contribution to our ministry from my first encounter with *Overseers of the Flock* to the classrooms for speech and Bible, to the altar at NBC where both of you prayed for the healing of our deaf

daughter, Melissa, to the 1980 General Assembly where you both
so graciously remembered our faces and our names. Thank you
for what you have done.

> With love and comfort,
> Dennis and Sharon Frey, *Pastor*
> Sterling, Ill., First Church
>   of the Nazarene
> NBC Graduate

And this letter from Gary Scarlett, pastor at Euless, Tex.,
was received shortly before Gideon's death:

> My life was indelibly changed by the Bible college. Of
> course, I went there to learn, and learn I did. But more than
> just learning, I was able to sit at the feet of some of the most
> godly people on this earth. Doctor G. B., I want you to know
> you had a profound influence on my ministry. "Preach the
> Word," you boomed. And I do, to the best of my ability. Your
> book *Holiness for Every Day* is my daily companion. I hear
> your voice and I sense your spirit each and every day.
>
> Our paths probably will never cross again on this
> earth, but Doctor, will you give me audience in eternity for
> a few thousand years? I want to be able to tell you what you
> have meant to me.

When it became clear that our work at Nazarene Bible
College was completed, we moved to Mesa, Ariz., in the summer
of 1980 to be near our son John, who became our pastor. Before
we left Colorado Springs, plans were made that we should return in the fall for a special occasion. The Board of Trustees had
voted several years prior to this that the Student Union Building
should be named Williamson Center, and it was decided that the
time had come for this honor to be bestowed. On October 28, this
was done in a very beautiful ceremony planned by President
L. S. Oliver. The featured speaker was General Superintendent
Eugene L. Stowe, who eloquently filled his place on the program.
Joseph, our elder son, came from Boston to be present for the
ceremonies. Maylou and Franklin Cook were there and John
and Chris Williamson. It was a memorable occasion.

On the preceding Sunday evening at Colorado Springs First Church, at the invitation of Pastor Melvin McCullough, Gideon preached what proved to be his last sermon from the text Eph. 2:20-22: "[Ye] are built upon the foundation of the apostles and prophets, Jesus Christ himself being the chief corner stone; in whom all the building fitly framed together groweth unto an holy temple in the Lord: in whom ye also are builded together for an habitation of God through the Spirit." Our family members all participated in the service and it was a victorious occasion. Gideon's voice was strong and his delivery animated. He was in the hospital before midnight that evening with severe internal bleeding, no doubt induced by the exertion of preaching. But he never felt that that last message had been too costly.

And so ends the saga of Gideon Williamson's relationship to Nazarene Bible College. He was instrumental in its founding; he gave his last full measure of devotion to its development and progress. He loved it deeply. He prayed thousands of prayers, many of them through the night, that it might fulfill God's purpose in its establishment. But when his day was done, he totally released it to God and to those appointed to carry on. He had done his best. Burden and responsibility were no longer his.

William Shakespeare declared:

> *There is a tide in the affairs of men*
> *Which, taken at the flood, leads on to fortune;*
> *Omitted, all the voyage of their life*
> *Is bound in shallows and in miseries,*
> *On such a full sea are we now afloat,*
> *And we must take the current when it serves,*
> *Or lose our ventures.*

Gideon prized a letter received from Louise R. Chapman, stalwart missionary and wife of the late General Superintendent James B. Chapman, under date of July 10, 1980. She wrote:

> One of the wisest and most fruitful things the church has ever done was to establish our Bible college at Colorado Springs.

We would never have had this institution had it not been for you.

I shall never forget your brave act when you left your place as a general and courageously walked down to exercise your privilege as a layman in the defense of the Bible college.

We were afloat on the full tide. You plunged into the flood and led us to fortune. Had you not done it, we probably would never have had our school.

I was proud of you that day. I can still see you as you obeyed God.

What marvels God has been able to perform for our church because of our Bible college. God bless you.

An appropriate conclusion to this chapter is an abridgement of the message given for Gideon at the college memorial service January 7, 1982, by Professor Janet Williams of the faculty. She said:

I first knew him as president of Eastern Nazarene College regarded with respect by his faculty and with awe by the students. He had gone to the college in 1936—depression days, to a college deeply in debt, faced with insolvency, threatened with bankruptcy. During his nine-year tenure, he miraculously restored it to financial stability. Bertha Munro, then dean of the college, said, "The president's resolute optimism and winning personality were made for the hour. His prayers of petition and thanks, his sense of vocation and dependence, all made him God's instrument. He was God's man for the crisis—His first words and his last were: 'God is able.'" When he left to be a pastor in Kansas City, the college was financially sound, fully accredited in the New England Association of Secondary Schools and Colleges, and trusted and supported by the entire constituency. He had the respect and confidence of students, faculty, churches, and pastors.

He exerted strong leadership in the affairs of the general church, never afraid to speak his mind, and not hesitating to push ahead any plans for which he felt God's leadership. There are those who criticized him for that day when he left his platform position and came down to the floor of the General Assembly to make an impassioned plea for a Bible college—a college that was to train for the pastorate the hundreds of older men and women, married with families, to give them an alternative to the home study course. He always believed in an educated ministry. Perhaps—yes, or maybe no—he did on that day envision a Bible college set on a hill from which men and women, called of God have gone forth to labor in the Church of the Nazarene, so that now one out of every five of our pastors in the United States are NBC graduates. Dr. G. B. Williamson was out in front—usually 25 years ahead of his contemporaries, and when he had a vision of something he felt was of God, he was adamant, almost reckless, in regard to place of position, putting himself on the line to fulfill those visions.

So he came to Colorado Springs—to teach the Bible and to be the chaplain. Did you know his contract called for him to be paid one dollar a year! I never heard him complain, nor did I ever hear him say he was tired—as many of us do. He mellowed much in his years among us. He loved us all and yearned for our successes.

Perhaps it was his years here that contributed to his devotional book *Holiness for Every Day*, the summary of his holy and godly life.

I shall remember him with awe—as my college president and presiding general.

I shall remember him as a man of integrity, paying the price of unpopularity for a school he felt was God's course.

I shall also remember the twinkle in his eye, especially in the love and devotion he had for his wife, Audrey—and for the firm recognition he always gave to her talents, abilities, and power with God.

I shall remember his concern for individual needs, not only in hospital calls, but in the hallways of this institution, down to his last days.

As Elishas, we wait below to take up his mantle.

**GIDEON:** Farewell
To the Church
To His Family
To Mortality

# FAREWELL
# TO THE CHURCH

Gideon began attending General Assemblies in 1928 and was a voting and vocal member of the General Assembly continuously from 1932 until 1980, thirteen in all. He believed in the authority of this body and accepted its decisions without protest, even where they ran counter to his own opinions. I often heard him say, "Let the General Assembly settle it."

Though he was ill, he wanted very much to attend the assembly of 1980, and this he was permitted to do. Dr. Orville W. Jenkins, general superintendent, invited him to give the opening devotional on the Thursday morning of that assembly. He quoted the following scriptures from memory:

"Christ . . . loved the church, and gave himself for it; that he might sanctify and cleanse it with the washing of water by the word, that he might present it to himself a glorious church, not having spot, or wrinkle, or any such thing; but that it should be holy and without blemish."

"Now therefore ye are no more strangers and foreigners, but fellowcitizens with the saints, and of the household of God; and we are built upon the foundation of the apostles and prophets, Jesus Christ himself being the chief corner stone; in whom all the building fitly framed together groweth unto an holy temple in the Lord: in whom ye also are builded together for an habitation of God through the Spirit."

"According as he hath chosen us in him before the foundation of the world, that we should be holy and without blame before him in love."

"And he gave some, apostles; and some, prophets; and some, evangelists; and some, pastors and teachers; for the perfecting of the saints, for the work of the ministry, for the edifying of the body of Christ: till we all come in the unity of the faith, and of the knowledge of the Son of God, unto a perfect man, unto the measure of the stature of the fulness of Christ."

Listen to Paul as he prays:

"And this I pray, that your love may abound yet more and more in knowledge and in all judgment; that ye may approve things that are excellent; that ye may be sincere and without offence till the day of Christ; being filled with the fruits of righteousness, which are by Jesus Christ, unto the glory and praise of God."

Let us pray as he prayed:

"For this cause I bow my knees unto the Father of our Lord Jesus Christ, of whom the whole family in heaven and earth is named, that he would grant you, according to the riches of his glory, to be strengthened with might by his Spirit in the inner man; that Christ may dwell in your hearts by faith; that ye, being rooted and grounded in love, may be able to comprehend with all saints what is the breadth, and length, and depth, and height; and to know the love of Christ, which passeth knowledge, that ye might be filled with all the fulness of God. Now unto him that is able to do exceeding abundantly above all that we ask or think, according to the power that worketh in us, unto him be glory in the church by Christ Jesus throughout all ages, world without end. Amen."

That's my prayer for you all.

And he added, "I don't expect to see you in Anaheim at the next General Assembly. I hope to have 'come to Mount Zion, and unto the city of the living God. To the general assembly and church of the firstborn, and to God the Judge of all and to the spirits of just men made perfect, and to Jesus the Mediator of the new covenant and to the blood of sprinkling that speaketh better things than that of Abel.' And so with warmest affection and sincere prayers and love for everybody, I bid you an affectionate farewell."

# FAREWELL TO HIS FAMILY

We were married June 6, 1931, in the Methodist Church, Oskaloosa, Ia. Here with the familiar background of the college where we both had graduated and where I had taught for 11 years, we plighted our troth. We were surrounded by the beautiful gladioli, peonies, and bridal wreath that an Iowa June can produce and by the love of hundreds of students and friends of many years. As we drove away on our honeymoon, a deluge of rain poured down on our secondhand Pontiac. As I drew up close to my bridegroom, I remember thinking, "Come rain or come shine, I am doing what I want to do." We had our measure of both rain and shine, but I never changed my mind.

Gideon wanted very much to celebrate our 50th wedding anniversary, and I shall be eternally grateful that we were permitted to do so. His worsening state of health forbade any public observance of the day. But our children planned a beautiful celebration strictly for the family. A bountiful dinner was served in a private dining room at the Phoenix, Ariz., Biltmore Hotel with candlelight and flowers, and with all the children and grandchildren present save one, we exchanged our vows:

"For better, for worse, for richer, for poorer, in sickness and in health, to love and to cherish, till death us do part."

They meant more than they had 50 years before. Gideon replaced the little worn, misshapen wedding band that had never been off my finger in 50 years with a new golden one inscribed with the dates and the words, "1931 More Love 1981." It is a solace to me now.

We received beautiful letters and cards from hundreds of friends, among them a lovely album from NBC alumni. Treasures they are to me now and a source of vast comfort.

On the following day, June 7, 1981, Gideon attended church for the last time. The people of Dobson Ranch Church of the Nazarene honored our Golden Wedding Day with appropriate ceremony and an elegant gift. Then our Joe preached at John's invitation in his pulpit. It was Pentecost Sunday, and we truly experienced a renewal of Pentecost as the Word was preached. After the service, when we were seated in the car, Gideon turned to Joe and said, "Let now thy servant depart in peace, for mine eyes have seen the King, the Lord of hosts." It was an emotion-packed moment for both.

Joe expressed his feelings about the event in the birthday card he sent his dad a few months later on November 26, 1981. He wrote:

> November is moving right along. That means once again the happy conjunction of Thanksgiving and your birthday. The timing of those celebrative events could not be better.
>
> It seems right to be explicit about that. So I want to say it clearly now that much of that for which I am grateful this year is what you have given me. All that is focused by the last two times we have been together, a year ago in Colorado, then at the time of the golden celebration in Arizona. I shall always be glad that in Colorado I heard you preach and in Arizona you heard me. Our shared attention and our shared vocation keep me proud and humble at the same time. We are a pretty good tandem as a matter of fact. I shall always know that and claim that.
>
> Thanks be to God. Thanks be to you. With more love than I can ever tell,
>
> Joe

Gideon died at 5:30 on the morning of December 30, 1981. He was very weak, as he had had no food for nine days. Though he did not speak, he seemed to be aware of my nearness and to be grateful for that.

I was up much of the preceding night, checking on him, and at 4 a.m. I dressed. I had been alone with him each night without any sense of fear, but on the preceding evening Maylou had said to me, "I'll be up to spend the night with you." And she was.

Several times as the hours passed, I was conscious of her presence and now as the end drew near for Gideon, Maylou was with me, though I had not called her.

The struggle to breathe abated as life ebbed away, and the end was peaceful and serene.

Maylou immediately slipped on her robe and went into action on the telephone. She dressed that evening, 12 hours later. I was grateful for her presence and her help, as well as for that of the other family members who so staunchly stood by me at this time.

The words of Scripture and of the old hymns were of unspeakable comfort to me in the long days of Gideon's illness. Lines from literature memorized many years before also were recalled. Words from Longfellow's "Evangeline" sustained me as I cared for my beloved:

> *Patience, accomplish thy labor, accomplish thy work of affection*
> *Sorrow and silence are strong, and patient endurance is God-like;*
> *Therefore accomplish thy labor of love, till thy heart is made God-like;*
> *Purified, strengthened, perfected, and rendered more worthy of heaven.*

It seemed it was I who had the lessons to learn. He was already prepared for heaven.

And that morning when he was gone, I repeated to God and
to his memory these words also from Longfellow's "Evangeline":

> *All was ended now, the hope and the fear and the sor-*
> *row,*
> *All the aching of heart, the restless, unsatisfied longing,*
> *All the dull deep pain, and the constant anguish of pa-*
> *tience!*
> *And as she pressed once more the lifeless head to her*
> *bosom,*
> *Meekly she bowed her own, and murmured, "Father, I*
> *thank Thee."*

And I did just that.

# FAREWELL MORTALITY

*Farewell, mortality; Jesus is mine!*
*Welcome, eternity; Jesus is mine!*
*Welcome, O loved and blest!*
*Welcome, sweet scenes of rest!*
*Welcome, my Saviour's breast!*
*Jesus is mine!*

Even as the death on the Cross loomed ahead of Jesus as He neared the end of His earthly sojourn, so Gideon Williamson saw Death coming toward him and made his preparation to meet this last enemy.

He first was aware of the malignancy in 1977. He went through 40 radiation treatments with courage and equanimity. Few people ever knew of his diagnosis, and for two and one-half years he pursued his natural way of life; teaching, preaching, and traveling as called upon to do so.

But in October of 1979, his condition changed drastically and rapidly. He was unable to go to his classrooms at Nazarene Bible College during the school year of 1979-80, and he was in the hospital numerous times. I believe now that he recognized that his illness was to be fatal unless God intervened. He spent many quiet hours coping with that idea. He earnestly searched the Word. Every page of his Bible shows use and perusal. He followed all the scriptural injunctions to obtain healing. He called for the elders of the church who anointed him with oil in the name of the Lord. It was a victorious occasion. But physical healing did not come.

As he reached the point of total commitment to what was

evidently the Father's will, it was almost as though he experienced a personality change. He had always been out in front, a man of vigor, aggression, energy, and contagious enthusiasm. Now he became quieter, more introspective, and above all, totally submissive.

The words of Katharina von Schlegel's seventeenth century hymn sustained him:

> *Be still, my soul; thy God doth undertake*
> *To guide the future as He has the past.*
> *Thy hope, thy confidence let nothing shake;*
> *All now mysterious shall be bright at last.*
> *Be still, my soul; the waves and winds still know*
> *His voice who ruled them when He dwelt below.*

In the fall of 1980, he began to experience great difficulty and pain in walking and even in sitting. I am sure now that long before the doctors pinpointed the fact that the malignancy had metasticized to the bones of the back, he knew he would not recover. Courageously and without a word of complaint or even question, he saw Death stalk toward him. He never flinched for a moment. With resignation and fortitude he accepted each growing weakness as it overtook him.

His death was not redemptive as was the Savior's, I know. And yet to those of us who stood by and watched him die, it was a purging, cleansing, awesome experience. I tried to be brave, but sometimes as I ministered to him, I would be overcome with emotion as he visibly failed. I can see his lips yet forming the words, "Don't cry!" even when the words were inaudible. He was looking beyond the suffering of this present time, to the glory that should be revealed.

Looking back, we, his family, have cause for gratitude. He traveled several millions of miles from mule-back to jet, yet was never in any known or immediate danger. He never lost a piece of luggage, never missed an appointment or had any serious delay. He was in Nicaragua at the time of a political coup, and in

Athens at the time of the revolution. He got out of Israel 15 days before the Six Day War. But he was kept in perfect peace.

I made only two requests of God as the illness progressed, that if possible, he might be spared the intense suffering we had been assured could accompany the final days; and the second, that I might be able to care for him myself in our own home where he so longed to be. God granted these two favors, and I shall be eternally grateful. The support of our family was of inestimable comfort to us both. I cannot thank them enough.

God's Word was unspeakably precious to us. I read to Gideon by the hour as long as his worsening condition permitted. This is a treasured memory.

And now, perhaps the most fitting way to close this chapter and to end this story is by repeating some lines from John Greenleaf Whittier's poem "The Eternal Goodness." I have heard Gideon quote them many times. He lived by the faith they express:

> *I know not what the future hath of marvel or surprise,*
> *Assured alone that life and death His mercy underlies.*
>
> . . . . . . . . . . . . . . . . . . . . . . . . . . . . . . . . . . . . . . . . . . . . . .
>
> *And so beside the Silent Sea I wait the muffled oar;*
> *No harm from Him can come to me on ocean or on*
> *    shore.*
> *I know not where His islands lift their fronded palms in*
> *    air;*
> *I only know I cannot drift beyond His love and care.*

He is at Home with the Lord he adored and did his best to serve. His absence leaves a lonesome place against the sky. But to change the figure, he would want no "moaning of the bar." He would challenge us all, as he did the last time he ever preached, to "Build the Church" until our summons comes!

"So passed the strong heroic soul away"—Tennyson.